AF244080

The Winning Zone

by
Al Smith, C.Ht.

Bloomington, IN   authorHOUSE®   Milton Keynes, UK

AuthorHouse™
1663 Liberty Drive, Suite 200
Bloomington, IN 47403
www.authorhouse.com
Phone: 1-800-839-8640

AuthorHouse™ UK Ltd.
500 Avebury Boulevard
Central Milton Keynes, MK9 2BE
www.authorhouse.co.uk
Phone: 08001974150

First published by AuthorHouse 9/18/2006

ISBN: 0-7596-6655-5 (sc)

Printed in the United States of America
Bloomington, Indiana

This book is printed on acid-free paper.

Alvin Smith understands that our lives are influenced so profoundly, yet so unnoticed, by our sub-conscious processes. This book is a marvelous collection of tools anyone can use to get the immense power of the subconscious working to carry out their conscious desires.

> *John G. Kappas, Ph.D.*
> *Founder, Hypnosis Motivation*
> *Institute*

I have continued to reach my goals in business and life as a result of the methods and training of Mr. Smith. It's like flying on autopilot.

> *Lynn A. Luna*
> *Vice President, Business Loan*
> *Support Manager*
> *Bank of America*

Table of Contents

Introduction ix

Chapter 1 SUBCONSCIOUS MIND POWER 1

Chapter 2 POWER TOOLS FOR HAPPINESS 6

Chapter 3 SELF HYPNOSIS 13

Chapter 4 HORSE SENSE 26

Chapter 5 STRESS REDUCTION 32

Chapter 6 STOP SMOKING NOW 39

Chapter 7 I'M TOO DARN FAT 48

Chapter 8 DESENSITIZING PHOBIAS 56

Chapter 9 BECOME YOUNG NOW 62

Chapter 10 CAN YOU BE HAPPILY MARRIED? 67

Chapter 11 YOU MAKE ME CRANKY 74

Chapter 12 WAKE UP AND GET REAL!!! 81

Chapter 13 PREDATORS 88

Chapter 14 FALSE CRUTCHES 94

Chapter 15 SPORTS PSYCHOLOGY 100

Chapter 16 LETS BE PALS 110

Chapter 17 LET'S GET RICH 119

Chapter 18 INTERNET ROMANCE 126

Chapter 19 RUBBING YOUR MAGIC LAMP 135

Chapter 20 GOD SMILES 142

Chapter 21 PROGRAMMING FOR SUCCESS 149

Epilogue 161

Introduction

Happiness is not a destination. It is a method of life.
- Burton Hills

For many years we have heard athletes refer to an exceptionally fine performance they had experienced as having played in the *Zone*. "I was playing in the zone," became a frequently used expression. They described this condition as a feeling of euphoria wherein every action seemed automatic and effortless. They had no concept of how they reached this state or even what that condition was. The athletes reached this level of performance only on rare occasions and were always trying to achieve that level again.

We now know that what they called the *Zone* was actually a state in which their ego or conscious mind was prevented from interfering with the subconscious control of their activity. This resulted in an automatic response of the proper muscles to the commands of the subconscious mind. This response occurred so rapidly that it felt fluid and unrestrained. I discovered how to produce the *Zone* level in an athlete over twenty-five years ago and have been teaching the method every since then.

Since producing the *Zone State* in sports was relatively simple, I found that it could be reproduced and applied effectively to nearly every human endeavor.

Living in the *Winning Zone* is much like flying on automatic pilot. Once the goals you wish to reach are correctly programmed into your inner mind the actions required to reach these goals become automatic and seemingly effortless.

I have aways been fascinated with the world of sports. Sports, to me are a reflection of life in microcosm. Athletics are based on rules, and these rules are based on the profound principles of life. These principles seem self-apparent and even though a sport is just a game as opposed to real life, it does serve as a beacon and a training ground for leading a happy and rewarding life.

A great deal of my life has been spent both participating in sports and in working as a sports psychologist with many athletes. I have a great respect for athletes both amateur and professional. The way they play their sport usually carries over into the way they live their lives for themselves and in the way they relate to other people.

I discovered that the same programs used for training athletes to achieve their top degree of performance could be easily and successfully applied to the improvement of everyone in the game of life.

Most of us have goals and desires we wish to reach. The methods outlined here will teach you how to get the results you wish in a very short time. The training is designed to instill in your mind powerful beliefs. Belief in one's self is the ultimate success in life and confidence is built on the foundation of belief.

This book condenses a great many ideas and effective programs into a guide that will help you enjoy life more fully. The fact that it simplifies subjects that could fill volumes required a great deal of thought and effort as well as the help of many generous friends in the field of mental reprogramming.

The underlying power I have stressed is belief. What a person believes about himself or herself in their subconscious mind is what that person will almost certainly become. We must rewrite the mental script in our subconscious mind to conform to the goals and desires we wish to achieve. We can become the person we want to be. We simply need to train our inner mind to these new beliefs.

Would you like to be truly happy? Do you desire to achieve greater success? You can. You will also experience a rewarding and enjoyable time in the process. Most people want to reach some kind of happiness and fulfillment in their own lives, but very few are fortunate enough to achieve it. Sadly, some people just don't believe they deserve to be happy.

We are often puzzled, when, after reaching a desired goal, with all the effort it required, that the ultimate attainment of the goal brought significantly less satisfaction than had been originally anticipated. This indicates that the goals chosen were not the goals that were dearest to our hearts and our own individual personalities.

The Winning Zone presents to you the proven methods and tools that will help you to avoid that sort of disappointment. There is a way to be truly happy, and by treating this pursuit like a game, it's really not that complicated and actually it's just a game that's fun to play. It's a game you will always win.

The Winning Zone was written to give you the power to become a happier, more successful person. Adding joy and direction to one's life is a goal well worth pursuing. Others developed many of the clear and sensible techniques described in the following chapters and they laid the foundation for the book. These various ideas and programs are the result of the research and practice of numerous great thinkers and teachers, ranging from doctors, clergymen, philosophers, psychiatrists, and even professional athletes.

I have simplified and organized these helpful discoveries in a way that everyone will understand so that they are able to apply them in their own daily quest for happiness. The chapters in this book are short and to the point.

I have practiced and taught these methods both as a sports psychologist and hypnotist for the past thirty years and I have seen these programs work effectively so many times for so many people, that I have no doubt that they will work for anyone who applies them in the course of their own life. The underlying theme: Happiness and Success, and how to achieve it. I hope you will enjoy reading and using this collection of useful methods to help improve your own happiness and success in life.

Anything that is accomplished in this life is first perceived and planned in the mind. Goals are set mentally before they can be physically accomplished. Unless these goals are believed to be achievable no progress will be made.

Remember the first time you fell in love? What feelings did that provoke in you? What felt good? What felt bad? What were you thinking? Were you thinking or just feeling? It really doesn't matter except to identify the true reason you felt happy. Rid your mind of the things that made you feel unhappy and concentrate on the things that made you feel good. Try and recall the last time you had a real belly laugh. What caused it? I bet you didn't have any thought of sadness in you head. That would have been impossible. Try to re-experience that event. Chances are you didn't feel foolish for laughing until your stomach hurt and the tears flowed and you felt happy.

Even after going through sadness or depression you can be truly happy and not feel guilty about it. If you know a person that enjoys being sad or seems to roll in self-pity, make a real effort to avoid being like he or she in your own life. This attitude is a crime against ones very self.

"If things were only different, if I had lots of money, if I was better looking, if I was healthier, if I had only married someone else, if I was just younger, then I would really be happy." Think again! You would still be unhappy because unhappiness is a bad habit, and there are many ways to get rid of bad habits. One of the best ways in the world to rid yourself of a bad habit is to replace it with a truly good habit.

The average person today doesn't know how to stop feeling miserable. They blame their distress on outside circumstances. The true reason for unhappiness lies in our own habit patterns. In order to change habit patterns a person must understand how to use the tools that the brain possesses. The brain utilizes similar tools to those of today's computer in that the computer is fed data to be stored, collated, disseminated etc... and when this is accomplished it will produce some sort of feedback. A similar type of collation and dissemination occurs with human beings after receiving sensory input or retrieving some stored feeling or event and this ultimately results in an inward or outward response that resembles the feedback the computer generates for us.

Regardless of the inward or outward response the information becomes stored away in the memory just as saved data remains stored on the computer's hard disk drive until the time comes to use, delete or replace it. The function of the computer was patterned after the manner in which the human brain functions.

The feedback that the computer provides, much like our own feedback, depends on the quality of the information received and stored. My first instructor on a computer said computers handle the transfer and arrangement of data. So if the data I loaded contained errors, the P.C. dutifully stored those errors and returned them to me when I asked for them or more simply put, *Garbage in, garbage out.*

Whether you have a P.C. or not, you are in the possession of the most powerful and accurate computer in the world: your brain. Just like the computer on the desk though, it stores information in much the same way, *garbage in, garbage out.* We need to monitor our own conscious input and evaluate the data we receive, eliminating the negatives and accepting the positives if we expect our brain to recover positive and accurate information and bring about happy self-confident feelings.

We follow this procedure because feelings are stimulated by the information stored in our brain. If you are feeling unhappy you have simply dredged up stored *garbage* that has no uplifting value.

People often permit negative input from others or even themselves to control how they feel both mentally and physically. The negative data that becomes stored in our mind can readily be replaced with more positive and happy beliefs that will enable us to take control over the way we choose to live.

When you use your key to access happy feelings you are retrieving the fun part of your life and enjoying the experience. Remember this very important key to being happy. *It is not the event, but what we believe about the event, that determines how we feel both rationally and emotionally.*

Instead of dwelling on the worst thing that could happen in your life, spend your time figuring out the best thing that could happen. The more positive thoughts, emotions and beliefs we store in the subconscious part of our brain, the more likely for us to bring out the happiest and most positive feelings into our daily lives. It sounds a bit like positive thinking. Positive thinking does play a role in the happiness process but the part it plays is far less powerful than our own positively planned mental reprogramming.

This book will teach you the proven methods and techniques of using the tools and methods described. These tools have been in use for quite some time and your success depends on the training and practice of a regimen that is easy, relaxing and actually fun to perform.

The Winning Zone Program will give you greater control of your emotions and will promote better health and vitality while at the same time you will be reducing stress and anxiety.

Everyone has their own personal genie to command and a winning zone in which they can perform. This genie's power is immense. The genie is the subconscious mind and to harness it's power just use the command tools in this book.

When we were young many of us dreamed of having an Aladdin's Lamp. When we rubbed this lamp a Genie would appear and grant us three wishes. I always thought my first wish would be to be granted at least a hundred more wishes.

We are all in possession of our own personal Genie. Since our Genie is our inner mind he is invisible to us. There is no limit to the number of wishes we can be granted. Our Genie takes his commands literally and we give these commands by vividly visualizing the outcome we desire as already accomplished. We must believe these goals are achievable. The subconscious mind, *Your Personal Genie,* is unable to differentiate between reality and your own vivid imagination so your commands commit him to action. Do not tell your Genie how to do his job. He will figure out the perfect method for reaching your goal. Hypnosis is the state in which we communicate with our Genie.

Once the vivid picture of the outcome you desire to reach has been instilled into your subconscious mind and reinforced to the point of total belief, the Genie goes to work twenty-four hours a day to achieve this programmed goal.

When you learned to walk, run or drive a car your subconscious mind took over the new task so well that you no longer needed to consciously try to control these actions.

As in training the muscles to perform a task automatically we simply train the mind to perform in happy, positive behavior patterns until this mental function and attitude becomes second nature. The subconscious will guide us to our desires and by not consciously interfering with the promptings received from our Genie we will be mentally and physically living successfully in the Winning Zone.

Put your own genie to work so that you begin achieving the goals you consciously desire. You will certainly become happier and more successful.

Chapter 1
SUBCONSCIOUS MIND POWER

The ultimate creative capacity of the brain may be, for all practical purposes, infinite.

- George Leonard.

In the early 60's a group scientists got together and devised the most advanced computer of its time. They fed in all the knowledge they could and started asking the most complicated questions, and the machine answered with ease. Then they asked it if there was a God. The machine responded.... "I do not compute." This was tried again in the 70's with more advanced technology. Finally, when asked if there was a God it replied, "I do not compute!"

In the early 90's scientists and programmers from around the world completed the most powerful computer on earth and programmed in all of the knowledge of mankind. When tested the machine responded in milliseconds with the correct answer to the most difficult questions they could devise. They finally asked the ultimate question..." Is there a God?" The computer whirred to life, the building shook, the sky darkened and the answer came forth..."There is now!"

As close as medical science has been able to measure, 88% of our brain functions as a great storage computer that we call the subconscious mind (the other 12% we refer to as the conscious mind). Stored in this computer we find every thought, experience and feeling we have been exposed to since our conception in our mother's womb. I also believe it holds the experiences and thoughts of our ancestors that have been passed down genetically.

To me this explains past life regression. Experiences not our own but commonly perceived as our own by those who dabble in regression and tend to believe in reincarnation.

The subconscious mind can store more data than all the computers of the world combined. A marvelous gift that when used properly can enrich our lives and help us to be happy, positive people.

Have you ever gone to sleep worried about a problem you needed to solve but seemed unable to? The subconscious has been given a search command and as it never sleeps, it continues to identify the problem and gather and collate all the information until it finds the solution. While your body was at rest the brain did all of the work. On awakening in the morning the solution came to your conscious mind and you were surprised how honest, practical and simple it was. You might wonder why you didn't think of that before?

As children our conscious mind (12%) is not fully developed. We call this part the judgmental brain. Before gaining its maturity a child's mind resembles a giant sponge soaking in knowledge as rapidly as the experiences or exposure to information occur. The child's mind does not judge the information and experience. The data just pours into the subconscious where it remains stored. Eventually the conscious mind starts to judge and question the data received.

All information received goes into what is called modern memory. Some of this data gradually becomes accepted and enters the subconscious for storage in the form of electrical charges called engrams. The data may be positive or negative or neutral. Once there it will always remain and can be recovered at a later date.

Since the cells of the brain are also in constant communication with one another, much like a man made computer, the information can be stored in many places at the same time. This means that such information can be retrieved rather easily. The information may be placed in what, in computer language has been termed the recycle bin, out of the way but retrievable.

For our purposes we can utilize this subconscious to reach our conscious desires. To work properly though, our goals must be clearly defined and totally accepted as reality. To achieve this we must employ all the senses: sight, sound, touch, taste and smell.

The subconscious mind does not differentiate between a real event and one that has been vividly imagined. The process of reprogramming the subconscious mind requires repetition and reinforcement.

Usually by the age of twelve the mind of a child has assimilated a tremendous amount of information. This little mind has learned to walk, talk, read and write, ride a bike, feed itself and so on. Most of this learning is necessary and positive. The majority of ideas and beliefs accumulated are for the good of the child.

Some beliefs however are negative and false and these will adversely influence the child for the rest of its life. Believing, as an example, that one can never be successful or that one is worthless or ugly or stupid will have a terrible effect on that individual.

Careless comments by parents, teachers, other children and even negative influences of movies and television will very likely set up a blueprint for unhappiness and failure.

Since the inner mind believes these negatives to be true, the individual will think and behave in a manner that fulfills these erroneous beliefs. Even if we become consciously aware of these false beliefs our subconscious mind still clings to them as being the truth. In this regard we are all successful as we do achieve the beliefs that are scripted in our own mind.

Positive reprogramming of the subconscious mind must be wisely used and reinforced to overcome undesirable conditions. We can replace the negative beliefs with a life changing positive blueprint. By applying these powerful and positive methods properly we will truly enjoy a wonderful new direction and control in our lives. We will become the person we really wish to be. We will achieve the success and happiness that had been stifled by the negative blueprint in our inner mind.

The most effective method of doing this is through subliminal suggestion, which is a technique of presenting ideas so rapidly that the conscious mind fails to comprehend that a suggestion has been given and therefore lacks the ability to judge or interfere. Visual subliminal suggestions using some medium, usually videotapes provide the most powerful and immediate results but for our purposes we will use self-hypnosis and focus more on the auditory and visualized reprogramming suggestions.

While not as powerful as the visual subliminal suggestions, auditory and visualized suggestions have proven extremely effective when used in conjunction with hypnosis.

Hypnosis compares to a state of meditation and deep relaxation. With practice you will be able to heighten your visualization to a point that it will become a very effective tool for programming the subconscious to believe that you have already reached your desired goal.

Unlike hypnosis, meditation usually dredges up feelings and ideas from past experience, similar to psychoanalysis.

Self-hypnosis can be used to deal with those feelings, anxieties and needs, and provide you with more control of your life giving you a stronger belief in yourself.

Self-hypnosis is used following a definite plan to actively program our computer for a specific purpose. In other words we are not searching for answers. We are giving definite, clear-cut commands in a very positive way. The relaxed feeling seems almost the same but the purpose is entirely different. We will be focusing on the achievement of goals from the perspective that the end result you are seeking has already been achieved.

Now things really begin to happen. Awake or asleep, your subconscious mind will gather and collate all the pertinent information to cause this goal to be realized. You may get the urge to call a particular person or go to a certain place or read a certain book. Whatever promptings you may have, cooperate with them. They are messages from your subconscious, suggesting the things you need to do in furthering yourself toward your desired goal. It is amazing how the inner computer works by putting data together and prompting you to take logical actions. These are the proper actions or responses that you may not be consciously aware of but this computer works for you when you are faced with a situation, event or feeling that requires some kind of action to be taken.

The more you practice this program, the more rapidly you will progress. In many cases I have seen, results have been reached in such a short time that it appears to be magic.

In the pursuit of happiness you will discover that hypnotic visualization will accelerate the achievement of your goal. The visualization of the goal as already being accomplished will cause it to become a reality. You will be able to do this again and again with any objective you truly want to achieve.

Chapter 2
POWER TOOLS FOR HAPPINESS

We used tools in the past to leverage our muscles. We use tools today to leverage our minds.

- Bill Gates

When any craftsman sets out to do a job he always makes sure he has the best tools with him. Tools are mans invention to make his work easier and more efficient. In the task of changing our lives and our self-image for the better we also need the best tools we can get. We do not necessarily need to use all of the tools at one time but when we need them we had better have them. I have selected what I believe will be the most essential and useful tools to help in beginning to generate positive life improvements. I want to keep this as simple as possible and in other chapters you will be told which tools are best suited for the work at hand.

1. Self Hypnosis

Self-hypnosis will be our main tool. This process will be used for programming and deprogramming our minds. A full chapter is devoted to the understanding and method of using this tool.

2. Audio Hypnosis Tapes

These tapes can be very useful but they are usually targeted for one specific goal, such as weight reduction, stress reduction, sports, stopping smoking etc. There are many fine tapes available. Following are some recommended companies that produce and distribute hypnosis tapes.

Potentials Unlimited
9390 Whitneyville Rd
Alto MI 49302
Hypnotist, Barrie Konicov

Golden Era
225 Pajaro Ave.
Ventura CA 93004
Hypnotist, Alvin Smith

Hypnosis Motivation Institute
18607 Ventura Blvd. Suite 310
Tarzana, CA 91356
Founder, John G. Kappas, Ph.D.

3. Subliminal Video Tapes

These tapes are also targeted toward specific goals. Subliminal videotapes are very effective. As you watch the tape you are seeing restful and beautiful scenes of the ocean or mountains, meadows and sky. In a multitude of small clips spaced throughout the tape are powerful suggestions that flash on the screen for less than a thirtieth of a second each. The conscious mind, unable to recognize these, allows these messages to go directly into the subconscious without any judgmental interference. Visual subliminal suggestion proved so powerful that the U.S. Government has outlawed its use in advertising. To obtain these tapes I recommend the same three companies listed for audiotapes. These are of excellent quality and content.

4. Medical Assistance

I have always believed that your physician should be consulted before engaging in any diet or exercise therapy. Sometimes the doctor may locate a medical problem that may contribute greatly to ones poor perception of himself. Do not overlook the contribution of medical science to helping you live a fuller, happier life. Locate a doctor that you can relate to and rely upon.

5. Positive Thinking

Consciously thinking in a positive manner plays a significant role as a great aid to reinforcing our new concept of ourselves.

Constantly thinking and repeating positive and happy thoughts has proven to be a very direct way of elevating our moods. There are many good books on this subject.

- **The Power of Positive Thinking, Norman Vincen Peale**
- **The Magic of Believing, Claude Bristol**
- **Psychocybernetics, Dr. Maxwell Maltz**
- **Success is not an Accident, John G. Kappas**

6. Other People

Some people are just great to be around. I'm sure you know at least a few. These people are always happy, sincere, positive and very outgoing in their personalities. Most of them are always anxious to help others, and have the knack of being interested in the welfare of others. They are unselfish, friendly, open, and are wonderfully attentive listeners. Cultivate the friendship of this type of person. Bask in their sunshine and absorb their good traits as much as you can. Avoid being around negative, pessimistic people. They always seem to be sad and gloomy. They are usually unsuccessful in life. Their advice will prove of no value to you, so do not listen to them. In fact, they may be a detriment to your happiness. These people take pleasure in bringing others down to their unhappy level. These are the folks that are the first to tell you that whatever you want to try is doomed to failure. They quickly find a dark side to everything. Do your very best to stay away from this type of person.

7. Goal Reinforcement

This program has been much overlooked by everyone except the advertising media. Whatever enters the eyes has a definite effect on your own beliefs. Advertisers blast us with pictures that do affect our buying decisions.

Type or write messages to yourself that reinforce your goal. Paste them on your mirror, refrigerator and any place where you will see them often. Read them over and over and be sure that the messages clearly describe the result you wish to achieve as if you have already reached that goal. Always make them positive messages such as, "I now weigh (desired weight) pounds and this is the way I am right now!" Find a picture of yourself when you were thin and paste that along side the message. If you don't have one you like, paste a picture of your face on a picture of a body you would like to resemble and say, "This is me now!"

The more frequently you see these messages the more powerful will become the reinforcement of your desired goal, the goal you have been programming through the hypnosis sessions. The goal could be a new house or car or cash. Use the appropriate pictures and statements like, "This is my new house."

8. Exercise

Using physical energy promotes health, fitness and a feeling of well being. The use of this energy has a calming, positive influence on your psyche as well. Mild exercise such as walking is strongly recommended by most doctors for physical and mental health. Aerobics, weight lifting, swimming and any number of sports like tennis, racquetball etc… can also provide many pleasing results. Of course before you institute any regimen it is strongly recommended that you consult your physician to make sure these activities will not prove too strenuous or actually do you harm instead of good.

9. Diet

The proper diet helps improve your body and your mind.   Consult your doctor and dietitian to obtain the correct diet for you. Certain foods also aid in calming the mind and promoting the feeling of welfare. If we eat junk foods we are basically sapping our body of energy. Cookies and candy bars, for instance, provide a quick "sugar rush" but when the rush has ended we feel more lethargic than we did before we ate it. Eating a more balanced diet with fresh fruits and vegetables, grains, and foods providing protein will provide you with more vitality. Accompany this with the proper use of vitamin supplements that you and your doctor feel will be the most appropriate for you.

10. Hobbies

Hobbies are wonderful brain relaxers and also a fascinating way to spend your leisure time. Most happy people that I have known, have hobby's they enjoy immensely. Hobby's offer us an escape from many of the pressures that we all must face. Embracing something that brings you a sense of satisfaction or contentment can greatly reduce your anxieties and stress, while providing you with many hours of pleasure. Find something that you truly enjoy doing and start doing it. If you are already engaged in a hobby spend more time at it.

11. Rewards

Reward yourself in some way for the progress you make towards your goal; perhaps dinner at a fine restaurant, a movie or new clothes. Pat yourself on the back. Learn how to really like yourself. Discover how to be your own best friend.

12. Religion

Many religious people discover great solace in prayer and in attending church services. If you have a religious nature, use it to pray for yourself and for others. People who actually help and care for others seem to be the happiest of all people I have ever known. My own faith in God has sustained me through some of the most difficult times in my life and given me great joy and inner peace as well.

13. Pen and Pencil Therapy

In nearly every chapter I advise you to write down your thoughts and your goals. This habit of writing things down will be one of the most important activities you perform. Writing has a profound effect on your subconscious mind both in programming and learning more about your real inner self. In chapter 19, I describe in detail how this practice will accelerate your goal achievement. These tools are all designed to improve your health and increase the amount of happiness in your life. Become familiar with these aids and use them as often as possible. Repeated reference to this section is greatly encouraged and you will discover that even the least significant sounding topics may help you derive the greatest benefit. Becoming a truly happy person involves a consistent effort. This effort will become second nature to you and therefore will eventually become an enjoyable practice.

14. Words are powerful.

An extremely useful technique is the use of a <u>tape recorder</u>. Using your known voice to change negative beliefs into positive useful beliefs will prove highly effective. By changing a negative belief we cause a great change in attitude which will cause a change in the way we feel. These new and good feelings will prompt us to react in a different way and these actions in turn produce wonderful results.

As far back as I recall I started to carry on conversations with myself in order to clarify my thinking. I began to pattern my work ethic after the great U.C.L.A basketball coach John Wooden. Wooden was a stickler for preparation in all things especially his team. His own high ideals, dignity and commitment fit my personality. I tape recorded my thoughts and tried to memorize them. Suddenly a light went on. Play the tapes back and listen over and over. I designed programs for specific needs like smoking, weight reduction and self esteem. It worked like magic, just let the tapes play and listen. How simple.

Chapter 3
SELF HYPNOSIS

Always have a plan, and believe in it. Nothing happens by accident.

- Chuck Knox.

THE TECHNIQUE USED TO CHANGE OUR INNERMOST BELIEFS ABOUT OURSELVES WILL BE THE USE OF SELF-HYPNOSIS. THERE IS MAGIC IN BELIEVING. IN FACT, WHAT WE TRULY BELIEVE, DIRECTLY INFLUENCES OUR EMOTIONS AND ACTIONS.

There is nothing abnormal about hypnosis; it is so common that the average person enters the hypnotized state approximately sixteen times each day. When you are engrossed in a book, TV show or movie, you are in a mild state of hypnosis already. On a long drive our minds drift into that state as well. Sometimes we even pass through a town without consciously realizing we have done so.

In order to achieve goals we must program our subconscious mind to believe we have already accomplished the goal we seek. We do this by vividly visualizing ourselves in that position. For the visualization to be most successful, it must incorporate all the senses of sight, sound, smell, touch and taste.

We make the end result so vivid and real that the subconscious mind finally accepts the goal as reality. When this has occurred the subconscious prompts us to do all the necessary things to make that goal a reality in our lives.

Self-hypnosis is a tool by which we can program our mind to the new belief about ourselves. It helps by awakening and focusing the senses to be used to implant a real and powerful suggestion into the subconscious computer. In fact the subconscious mind does not pass judgment and lacks the ability to differentiate between a real event and one that we vividly imagine.

After constant repetition under hypnosis, the new belief becomes deeply imbedded in our minds. Our behavior patterns and conscious thoughts make the needed adjustments in our actions in order to cooperate with our new belief about ourselves.

As an example let's use what I refer to as possibility thinking. Most people tend to think of the worst thing that could happen regarding circumstances (negative). Instead, imagine the very best thing that could happen (positive), because this choice is just as likely to occur. When we have programmed our minds to use the latter described attitude we will become more positive and happy thus reducing stress. This attitude must become a true belief so that we automatically tend to think of positive results.

Remember all the negative outcomes that you imagined that have never occurred. All of us at different times expended unnecessary energy expecting the worst outcomes when in fact they never came about.

Avoid the worry and imagine all of the good things that may occur instead, ridding yourself of worry and stress. The good outcome is just as likely to happen, and with this attitude, good things will more than likely be the result. Even if things don't turn out well you have avoided a lot of anguish and reduced your stress level.

Although we cannot always control circumstances we can change the way we are affected by them by changing our attitude towards them. All successful happy people have this habit of always expecting the best. We should adopt this same attitude in our own thinking to the point of making it a habit pattern that will never leave us.

<u>How to Program the Mind.</u>

The subconscious mind operates non-judgmentally without regard to reality or fantasy so our programming begins by creation of a new self-image. Write down exactly the way you want to look, feel and behave and the other goals you wish to reach.

When you have completed your list examine it and assign priorities to the goals you wish to accomplish. One of your desired goals may be so minor that you feel you could reach it by just using your willpower.

I have found it a good practice for beginners to apply the visualization process to just such a minor goal. By doing this first you will not only be perfecting this technique but you will also begin building self confidence in it's application as well as achieving your desired result in a rather short time.

By attacking the smaller problem and discovering for yourself how well this method of programming works it will become easier for you to apply this technique to the more important issues.

Practice the self-hypnosis and visualization frequently until you have mastered this procedure. When each session is finished be sure to apply the arousal formula, 0-1-2-3-4-5 WIDE-AWAKE! WIDE-AWAKE! This is very important, as you do not want to remain in a state of suggestibility where you might be vulnerable to negative input from other sources.

One of the most important discoveries about the subconscious mind pertains to the fact that it never sleeps and that the subconscious mind performs in a similar way to a guided missile. This being so, the goal must be very clear and specific. For our purposes we implant suggestions, which the inner computer accepts as real and achievable. The goal must be seen in the mind as already accomplished.

Many of the wealthiest people in the world were from very poor families. Because of their lack of money, luxuries and security, these people while still very young, concentrated on the acquisition of wealth. While still in poverty they vividly imagined what it was like to live in a mansion, drive expensive cars, dress well, travel in style, etc.…

They pictured money coming into their hands, checks arriving, properties they owned and influential people as their friends, and so on. Their desires and fantasies became as real to them as reality itself. Under the influence of this imagination their minds were programmed to proceed just like the guided missile, causing their thinking and activities to ultimately lead them to the wealth they sought.

Children have the great capacity for imagination and as their judgmental mind has not yet fully developed their practice of play-acting a part will serve as a direct programming of their subconscious mind.

Ben Hogan, the famous professional golfer, told of the times when very young, of imagining the shots he was practicing as if they were actually shots he was making in a major tournament. He would vividly imagine the putt he was making was truly a crucial putt on which depended his winning the U.S. Open, or The Masters or even The British Open. He was visualizing and programming his mind for events in his career that later became reality.

I believe from the comments I've read about Mr. Hogan that he was playing tournaments in a state of mild hypnosis in which he was so focused on the outcome he desired that he was almost oblivious to the conversations of his playing partners. One famous professional when asked what Ben Hogan had said to him during their round, replied, "The only times he spoke to me was when he said, 'You're Away!'" This absolute concentration Hogan displayed was a habit of mental management he programmed into his subconscious mind at an early age.

It was said that Ben Hogan was such an accurate player that he would be hitting the golf ball out of the same divots he made during his previous round. His powerful ability to visualize led him to make the remark that he had clearly seen the shot and its outcome before he had even begun his back swing.

When you have set up a positive blueprint in your subconscious mind in regard to the goals you wish to achieve the actual belief in your performance will become just second nature to you.

This technology can be used successfully to reach any goal you desire to obtain. It is the number one tool in your toolbox and in the categories discussed in this book; it will be the primary tool to be used.

How Do I Induce Hypnosis?

Read and adhere to the following instructions, then practice them daily. Soon you will be able to reach the proper state for programming. Remember I said it was natural and it really is. Do not expect any strange things to occur. This is not Dreamland. It is a focused and relaxed state of mind wherein you will achieve the ability to vividly visualize your goals and wishes creating a firm foundation for goal achievement.

Regimen

Choose a room in which you feel comfortable and are unlikely to be disturbed or interrupted. Use a comfortable chair but not too comfortable. You don't want to fall asleep; you are here to work on programming the inner computer.

Let's begin. Loosen any tight fitting belts or clothing, kick off your shoes and shift around in the chair until you feel very comfortable.

There are certain words, which will produce a strong feeling within you. These key words vary with different people. In the following two sets of words pick out the one from each set which has the most significant influence on your feelings. Repeat each word to yourself twice. When you have found one word from each set that seems to be the most powerful, write them down. These will be your own key words from now on.

SET # 1

HEAVY WARM TINGLING LIGHT FLOATING NUMB

SET # 2

HAPPY CONFIDENT SMILE SUCCESS CALM PEACEFUL

Once you have discovered your key words, enhance them by picturing how they affect you. If the word in set one is tingling, then imagine a tingling sensation in your feet and toes, hands and fingers. Make these feelings as powerful as you can. Practice will improve this ability.

In set two if smile happened to be your key word, visualize the smile on a Cheshire cat and make the smile appear as big as a house then as big as the sky. Make it huge and powerful.

The third key is the same for everyone. Say to yourself, DEEP HYPNOTIC SLEEP. And DEEPER STILL and DEEPER STILL. Now count down 5, 4, 3, 2, 1, 0 then repeat DEEP SLEEP and DEEPER STILL.

With your eyes closed visualize a yardstick with very clear inch markings. It is standing on end and your eyes are very close to it, 36 inch mark at the top and 0 inch mark at the very bottom.

Visualize that you are lowering yourself down until you are clearly at the 18-inch mark right in front of your eyes. Now go up and down the depth of the yardstick. This lets you know that you are in complete control of the depth of your hypnotic state. When you are comfortable with this, find the depth at which you feel most at ease.

This is the place to begin your visualization and begin programming the self-image changing suggestions. The deeper you go the better the visualization will be and consequently the more success you will achieve. Some people do not visualize easily at first. It is just as effective to imagine the suggestions instead. Visualization will come after continued practice.

Tell yourself that each and every time you practice your session you will be able to reach your working state more rapidly and easily. Tell yourself that your visualization continually becomes more vivid and realistic. Program into your mind that you will sleep deeply and peacefully at night, and awaken refreshed and full of energy in the morning.

Work on only one specific goal at a time. Try to first visualize the desired outcome clearly and in color. See details such as skin texture, light, shadow, etc...everything aimed at making the experience real. Try to bring sound into the picture such as music, voices and background noises. Try to smell the aroma of the vision you are working on.

Feel the texture of the objects in this scene and then try to taste any object in the picture. This will require practice and will improve dramatically in time.

The objective is to promote this as a real experience to be absorbed by the subconscious mind, as it is unable to differentiate between reality and vividly visualized data. It stores this new positive experience and will begin to cooperate in procuring your objective. Since the subconscious part of our brain never sleeps it will store and collate this input and then devise the most efficient method of achieving the desired result. Constant repetition of this exercise will continue to strengthen and reinforce this new belief and cause the inner computer to adhere to the desire of the conscious mind.

You will over the next few weeks notice urges to phone some particular person or visit some certain place or perform some action without consciously knowing why. Do not fight these urges, rather cooperate with them as they are promptings from the subconscious to follow an extremely well devised plan formed by your inner computer.

These plans are organized and aimed at the results you want to achieve. The results will astonish you as everything starts to fall into place automatically and seemingly with very little effort. This is not magic. It is mental technology that works. Do not stop the programming sessions. Adhere to them on a regular basis.

With practice you will be able to reach this state of deep relaxation in less than a minute and do your visualization in less than five minutes a session.

When you first begin you may wish to use relaxation techniques to deepen your state.

Focus on your feet and toes and ankles and say to yourself. I am relaxing every muscle every nerve every tendon and every joint in my feet and toes and ankles. Concentrate your attention on these parts of your body and feel them let go and relax. Continue this procedure up through the calves, knees, thighs and hip joints, buttocks, abdomen, spine, torso, shoulders, neck, arms, elbows, wrists, hands, fingers and knuckles. Now spend time relaxing the neck, scalp, forehead, eyes, eyebrows, eyelids, facial muscles, jaws, tongue, nostrils, sinuses, ears and inner ears.

Keep your attention on these parts of your body and let them relax completely.

Tell yourself that all your organs are relaxing and that the respiratory, circulatory, digestive and nervous systems are all relaxing and functioning perfectly and in complete harmony. Finally the brain is addressed and caused to be calm and clear as if it were a lake with slight ripples on its surface. These ripples are just extraneous thoughts. Allow the ripples to calm and disappear, and see the surface of the lake become as still and clear as a pane of glass. Now you are able to see deep down into the clear lake of your mind and calm any activities there.

This exercise will greatly deepen your state of hypnosis and increase the effectiveness of your visualization.

Program the new beliefs about yourself into your inner computer and develop the behavioral and personality changes that are necessary to bring about the results you desire.

Be assured that you can waken from the hypnotic state at any time you wish. You will wake up instantly in the event of any emergency or anything that may require your immediate attention.

To come out of your session use the following procedure.

"I am waking up starting with my feet and legs, all feelings returning to normal, continue this up through your hips, torso, shoulders and arms. Then focus on your hands, neck, head and face.

"I am feeling fine, refreshed, and happy. I am in total control of my feelings and myself. Each and every time I do this exercise it will become easier and more effective. I will sleep well at night and awaken refreshed in the morning, full of energy and in a wonderful confident frame of mind. I will never go into a state of hypnosis unless it is my conscious desire to do so. I am now waking up starting with my feet and up through my legs and torso, arms, hands, neck and head. Feeling great and in a very happy state of mind. Now counting up 0-1-2-3-4-5- WIDE-AWAKE. WIDE AWAKE."

After bringing yourself to a full waking state stretch your arms and legs and take a few minutes to review your session and to remember how good it felt.

Resolve to practice this program daily to reinforce and strengthen the new inner beliefs you have programmed. Learn to enjoy the time you spend in programming. You are in charge of your life and your emotions. Do not allow others to have a negative influence on you. You are the one in control.

Be sure to memorize and practice what you have just read.

This process is much easier to perform than it sounds, and it is a natural function of your brain.

Use this technique to increase and prolong the feelings of inner peace and happiness. Recall the keys to your own happiness frequently, especially when in the state of hypnosis. This will tend to reinforce a happy, friendly, self-assured, personality.

When practicing self-hypnosis be sure that you have taken the time to examine the most important goals you wish to achieve. There will be a number of things you want to change about yourself. Write the changes down and really give them serious thought then assign them each a priority. As you read through your list you will discover that many changes you wish to make can be easily reached by simply making a rational decision to alter your usual activities.

In making these changes you may find it easy to just avoid being in situations that are conducive to the behavior you wish to change.

Being around certain people or places may lead you into activities or unpleasant thoughts you would rather avoid.

You can decide to stay away from these people and places and thereby eliminate the problems they cause in your life.

The self-hypnosis program is designed to be used for changing your own habits and personality traits that are already deeply ingrained in your subconscious mind. Reaching goals that you wish to achieve will require revamping your habits and personality traits.

Selecting the right goals for yourself is a very necessary part of the whole procedure.

It is important to write these goals down and decide which ones are most in need of the reprogramming techniques of self-hypnosis. Committing your goals to paper in your own handwriting will help you to clarify your thinking. Keeping a journal is an important method of learning to focus on the primary conditions you wish to change.

So many times we hold onto negative beliefs ingrained in the subconscious mind, which prevent us from achieving what we consciously desire for ourselves. This negative blueprint led us to where we are now. In that respect we have already become very successful as we reached the goals that were programmed long ago.

The self-defeating, negative blueprint has been the focal point of all our previous efforts. We must replace this negative blueprint with the positive beliefs and habits that will lead to our reaching the happier and more successful life we desire.

Our own inner beliefs about ourselves are similar to a river channel that we automatically follow. It is necessary for positive change to occur to develop a new river channel of belief.

Through repeated programming make it deeper than the negative channel we have been following thus diverting our old negative beliefs out of our life and placing our new and positive beliefs into this deeper, more powerful channel.

Through the use of self-hypnosis we train our subconscious mind to accept as true, positive new beliefs about ourselves, which will guide us to the happy life we wish to lead. This is the way we are able to quickly achieve the proper goals we have selected.

When first entering into this program you may find it of benefit to consult a certified hypnotist so that you will discover just what the state of hypnosis feels like to you.

The majority of people will find that this altered state of consciousness is something they have experienced many times in the past. The body will become very relaxed and the mind will become very clear and focused.

Usually when I work with a person I teach them self-hypnosis by the end of the third or fourth session. I believe it is preferable that the person learns to handle their own programming sessions and develop their personal control of the hypnotic state. This also gives a person the ability to powerfully reinforce the positive suggestions to their subconscious mind.

Self-hypnosis increases your power of self-control and strengthens your self-confidence. This is very important as you quickly learn to avoid accepting negative thoughts and suggestions from other people. You will become aware of the state of hypersuggetibility (hypnosis) and become able to retain alert, conscious control of your own mind.

In this age of being exposed to blizzards of information it is important to be able to discern the difference between positive and negative information that may have an effect on your own well being. Possessing this mental alertness will allow you to make rational and wise decisions that will only enhance the way you live. The reprogramming of the subconscious mind will prompt you to take certain actions.

These promptings will be messages from the subconscious mind that has developed a wise and well-designed plan of action, which will guide you to your goal.

In order to achieve total success it is absolutely necessary to take action. Follow the prompting of your subconscious. Take action and you will achieve the goals you have set for yourself.

25

Chapter 4
HORSE SENSE

Common sense is not so common.

- Voltaire.

Have you ever known anyone that seemed to have a real grip on life? If you have, try to analyze just what it was about that person that gave you that impression. Maybe it might have been a high I. Q. or perhaps the person you observed just used a lot of common sense. We have all known many people who had and used an abundance of common sense. I have always had a tendency to try and think creatively. Unfortunately, this often led to making decisions based more on emotion than on down to earth facts. Of course the world always needs creative thinkers and dreamers. Without them art would never have reached the heights it has. Even science would still be in the Stone Age unless we had people of vision who dreamed of accomplishing things that seemed at that time to be impossible.

In the day-to-day business of life however, the person of great common sense seems the most secure. They go about doing all the wise things that lead to success and happiness.

They make decisions based on facts, which they take the time to gather. Without the practical pigs of the world the dreamers would be lost.

Fortunately for me I married a very common sense lady. She was only seventeen years old and I was twenty-five. She had not even graduated from high school when I was finishing college. It took me years to discover that she was far wiser than I was. In every business decision in our life together, when we did what I was sure was the right thing, it failed. My wife proved to be nearly 100% correct about the paths we should follow. In spite of her lack of education she saw and clearly recognized reality.

Under her guidance and wisdom we raised four wonderful children and she actually managed to teach me the value of using common sense. She encouraged me to pursue the things I liked doing and stood behind me in all my personal endeavors. She taught me how to see life from her own firm foundation of common sense. I began to realize how truly wise she was. She would gently pull me back to earth and reality. I started to learn how valuable common sense could be. I began seeing people and situations from a new perspective. I learned to value and enjoy the simple things in life and stop chasing the rainbows I might never catch.

I learned to love our children in a real and happy way. Watching them grow up and discover things for themselves was a new delight. Learning what real love meant, bowled me over.

She always encouraged me to continue learning and worked hard to build my confidence in my role as a husband and father as well as a teacher of others. Had it not been for her deep human understanding and ability to lead from the background, I feel I would never have grown to my full potential. She let me keep my head in the clouds but made sure my feet stayed on the ground.

After our children had all graduated from high school and gone on to college she decided the time had come for her to have her diploma. She went to night school on her own and after her graduation; she entered medical training and became a nurse. She made me very proud. She waited and sacrificed until our children had finished school before she got her high school diploma. Attending her graduation made me feel even prouder of this woman with her simple and direct approach to life and her love for it. Fourteen years ago my wife died of cancer. She left a great legacy to all that knew her. She left the children with the gift of common sense and the will to persevere. Every day I try to emulate her sound common sense approach to life.

Common sense is basically using your head to think logically instead of emotionally. See things for what they really are and not what you wish they were. When you have all the pertinent facts regarding a decision to be made and avoid wishful thinking, then your decision will usually be the right one.

Emotion plays a very wonderful role in our lives. Love, sacrifice, compassion for others, appreciation of beauty and so forth are the appropriate grounds for emotion but we must always use our heads, our rational thinking brain.

You do not need to be well educated to use real common sense. You automatically know if something will be bad for you. If you encounter bad things, avoid them. When you know you have found something good and you have all the facts, embrace it.

As my wife and I grew together in love and understanding I began to apply the common sense principles to my career in golf and as a hypnotist and sports psychologist. When I work with people I insist we explore all the common sense solutions before going on to the mental programming. If you are feeling ill, go to the doctor. If you are having a spiritual problem, go to a priest or minister. If you are having an emotional problem, see a psychiatrist or counselor.

When you have reached the point where you wish to change the direction of your life, whether it is losing weight increasing self esteem or setting and reaching goals, you are more than ready to use the programs outlined in this book. If these programs and exercises were not based on facts and grounded in common sense they would not have any value. Through the knowledge of many competent researchers and practitioners I can assure you that these programs and exercises are solidly founded not only in fact but also very deeply in common sense.

It has been my privilege to have learned from and shared with professionals of both genius and compassion. As a plain old down to earth, country boy, hypnotist and trainer, I have been able to put on paper very complex truths and practices that will benefit everyone.

When I tell you that by using common sense you can avoid many of life's problems and solve many of life's difficulties, I speak as one who was trained by a master. I learned that happiness is being the person that enjoys life's little pleasures.

Reaching for goals and knowing you have done your best brings more happiness than the reaching of the goal. Anticipation itself, you will find, will prove as joy provoking as the actual realization of your desired goals.

It is wise to make a complete and honest examination of your strengths as well as your weaknesses. I find that it is a good practice to write these traits down. When you are able to see things you feel about yourself in black and white it becomes easy to locate the ones that make you feel worthwhile. It also becomes obvious that whatever shortcomings you have are not quite as bad as you have allowed them to affect you. Many character faults can be changed or removed with a little effort on your part. In fact some of the ones we look upon, as faults are really blessings in disguise.

The time you spend committing to paper the feelings and beliefs you have about yourself will lead you to some very obvious conclusions which were not really that apparent to you before. It is almost like being outside your own body observing things in an objective manner. It is only human to make mistakes and it is also human to forgive those errors. Many of us need to forgive ourselves for the many petty mistakes we have made in our lives.

The object of this exercise is to determine exactly what we like and dislike about our own personalities. We can then take an objective, unemotional approach to make the changes that will help us become the type of person we enjoy being around. This is not meant to be an exercise in self-love or in self-pity. It more closely resembles a concerted attempt at self-acceptance.

When we locate obvious flaws in our character we must make an effort to eradicate these flaws.

Using the Power Tools for Happiness chapter, we will pick out the correct approach to enable us to overcome our serious faults. The main purpose we are trying to accomplish is to become a person we can really like. Discovering our own finer qualities we concentrate on making them more important than the flaws in order to improve our self-respect. As this is always personal and confidential there is no need to feel awkward or embarrassed. We do not share these intimate discoveries with anyone else so let's not gloss over the truth. Other people have their own flaws to contend with.

When you develop the habit of being truly honest to yourself you will find a great burden has been lifted from your psyche. True self knowledge is power not only over your feelings but also directs you to an intelligent method of attaining power over outside circumstances and the way they affect you.

This practice will enable you to gather facts about your feelings and beliefs. Self-knowledge translates into powerful self-control. Clear, unemotional thinking opens the door to wise decision-making. In all your decisions you should gather all the facts available then examine these facts. The correct action for you then becomes very obvious.

Years ago when life was less complex than it is in today's society, people were able to naturally use common sense to guide themselves to a less stressful way of dealing with life. As we have allowed our minds to be overloaded with usually wasteful information we have forgotten how to see circumstances and emotions in a common sense way. This bombardment of high tech, negative input can be seen for what it really is when we rediscover how to return to our inherent ability to think clearly and unemotionally. We have this ability to adapt and overcome all obstacles to our own happiness and success.

Chapter 5
STRESS REDUCTION

Pressure and stress is the common cold of the psyche.
- Andrew Denton.

The stresses of modern day living have been directly associated with hypertension and heart disease along with numerous other illnesses. Stress looms as a condition that needs to be reduced and if possible eradicated. This condition focuses itself primarily on the sympathetic nervous system, or as I term it, the primitive mind, the old fight or flight syndrome, in which our reactions are restricted by our modern day society.

With nothing directly to physically fight or run away from we find ourselves in a catch twenty-two situation. The bombardment of negative input, noise, anger, discomfort, etc., directly affects the primitive mind causing the excess secretion of adrenaline while at the same time heightening the state of tension in the entire body. Tension of muscles, rapid heartbeat, heightened blood pressure; stomach discomfort and other very unpleasant symptoms often result from the exposure to, or the existence of stress.

The first and most important thing I recommend is to consult your physician. He will determine what medications and other treatments should be undertaken. Everything else I have to offer should be secondary to medical treatment and should be discussed with your doctor. Most physicians I personally know approve of the self-help methods I will describe and most other doctors will probably encourage you to follow one or more of these stress reduction techniques.

Stress from the job affects many people and happens to be considered one of the more prevalent causes. Unhappy marriages, fears, minor illnesses, living conditions, worry and lack of money, are just a few of the contributing factors to stress. Stress can be caused by almost anything and never think you are alone with your feelings or problems. Even some of the most famous and successful people in the world experience stress. We need to find what your stress points are and start offering them some relief.

<u>Common Sense Approach</u>

Try to determine the most stress producing elements in your life. Sometimes a complete change of lifestyle will significantly reduce stress. Maybe climbing the corporate ladder is not worth the cost to your health. Long commutes to work may be eliminated by finding an occupation closer to your home.

Living and working in the suburbs instead of living and working in urban areas may substantially reduce stress.

Clear, responsible and common sense changes are alternatives that you should examine and decide upon. Your doctor may recommend mild physical activity, which also tends to reduce stress both physically and psychologically. Becoming engrossed in a hobby totally unrelated to your employment can also be very beneficial. Other common sense decisions involve, but are not limited to; avoiding people, places, sounds etc... (Whatever the case may be) that upset your emotions.

There are important and various methods of assisting your doctor in helping to reduce stress and hypertension in your life. These are programs, which you can practice on your own. They have been proven effective over the years by psychiatrists, psychologists and hypnotherapists, to be very useful in reducing stress.

The most important things to know: are the true causes of the stress reaction. Clear thinking will be required to do this effectively. Writing the causes down on a sheet of paper aids in locating and defining the causes and their hierarchy. When you have them written down you can also make notes of ways in which to deal with them individually. A much-overlooked cause of stress is guilt. Everyone harbors some guilt feelings in his mind. Exploring feelings of guilt takes time and patience.

Writing these feelings down helps to clarify just how important they are and also the degree of power they possess in your mind to produce stress.

Understanding whether your guilt feelings are significant or even unimportant will assist you in relieving yourself of much of the pressure these feelings have generated.

In order to improve you need to learn to forgive yourself and learn to accept the forgiveness of others. When you examine what you have written regarding these feelings you bring to the surface of your conscious mind much supposed guilt that has no basis in reality. Insignificant guilt feelings placed in your mind by parents or teachers at an early age will be recognized as problem provoking and usually unfounded. See all guilt feelings in a new way and recognize them for what they truly are.

If there is reparation that you feel should be made, do what you can to rectify the damage you have caused others. If that is not possible, then do acts of kindness for others. You are not as bad as you may have thought you were.

Being human, we are all subject to the making of mistakes whether by intention or by accident. Recognize these guilt feelings as being common to all people. Forgive yourself and release the tension these feelings have caused. Tension (stress) sensitizes the nervous system and can surely lead to physical illness.

I believe the medical profession should pay far greater attention to the patient's psyche. Often doctors are wary of this as they feel they may be infringing in the realm of religion.

We as humans are not only physical but also we are psychological and spiritual in our nature. Many people I have known that deny the existence of God frequently blame God for the miseries they confront in life. This attitude expresses quite a contradiction. People have an inherent belief in fairness; they want the books of life to balance.

Guilt feelings are very significant in the causing of tension. These feelings must be addressed and resolved in order to help the physician reduce the condition of stress.

Great importance must be placed on realizing that what affects us emotionally is not so much a fact or an occurrence as it is our perception of that fact or occurrence.   In other words our perceptions may be a hundred and eighty degrees away from the truth.   These perceptions can be changed from negative to positive and truly improve our health and happiness.

Self Hypnosis

Self-hypnosis relies on the premise that the happy, positive goal must be believed without any trace of doubt. Significant importance should be placed here for here we form the foundation of recovery or self-betterment. When our primitive mind accepts as reality what we program, it will from that point forward guide us to that desired condition.

Using self-hypnosis we strive to reach a deep working state. We visualize or imagine ourselves as completely relaxed and calm and this visualization will be reinforced by the relaxed state of our body. Refer to chapter three and master this technique. Hypnosis is an extremely important tool, which will accelerate your healing progress.

Picture a tranquil scene and rest yourself in that particular environment, always making the visualization as real as possible by attuning all the senses to that particular state. Tell yourself that wherever you may be during the waking state you will remain calm and relaxed in your mind and body.

These sessions should be repeated over and over as the reinforcement of these suggestions strengthens that belief.

Some people are unable to achieve clear visualization. This is not totally necessary. You just need to imagine the scene and experience the relaxed feelings again and again until they become normal and natural reactions to you. After constant repetition you will begin to find this a normal expected feeling in your daily life.

Make yourself aware of the differing feelings of tension and relaxation in the muscles. The following exercises designed by clinical psychologist and hypnotist, Leslie Le Cron, will prove of great value in reducing stress.

The underlying principle is that a tired group of muscles will automatically relax when conscious attention has been diverted from them.

Exercise

Follow these steps, and within a few attempts, you will begin to gain solid ground in your efforts.

1) While sitting upright, move your head around slowly in a counter clockwise direction four times, then four times in a clockwise direction.
2) Now lie down on your back on a bed or sofa and take several deep breaths.
3) Now lift your left leg about a foot above the bed while making its muscles tight for about ten seconds. Focus your attention on the muscles and tendons in that leg.
4) Now, let it go completely limp and let it drop to the bed like a dead weight.
5) Immediately lift your right leg and go through the same exercise while focusing attention on the right

leg and ignoring the left leg entirely. The left leg will automatically go completely relaxed and stay relaxed. After ten seconds has elapsed, let the right leg drop and lift your left arm to a forty-five degree angle to your body.

6) Clench the left fist and make the arm muscles as tight as you can, making them as rigid as possible while focusing total attention on those muscles. While your full attention is thus diverted the right leg will achieve and remain in a total state of relaxation. Hold that arm rigid for fifteen seconds then allow it to drop to your side while raising the right arm and performing the same exercise with it, while focusing full attention to the tension in the muscles and tendons in that arm and diverting attention from the left arm allowing it to automatically relax.

7) When you let your right arm fall to your side and with your eyes closed, imagine a four-foot diameter circle on the ceiling and have your eyes follow the circle in a clockwise direction four times then follow the circle counterclockwise four times. Now change the circle into a square and follow the outline slowly in a clockwise direction four times then follow the outline of the square in a counter clockwise direction four times.

The mechanics of these exercises focus on diverting attention from the arms and legs allowing them to reach a deeper state of relaxation.

After practicing the exercise three or four times you will be able to reach the full benefit of the relaxed condition. Remember not to lower your legs and arms slowly. You must let them drop like dead weights to avoid storing any tension. In addition to achieving a deeply relaxed state, this exercise also helps to tone and firm the muscles being used.

When the exercise has been concluded continue to lie back for a while and enjoy the deep state of relaxation.

<u>Transcendental Meditation</u>

Doctor's Herbert Benson and Robert Wallace conducted exhaustive studies of practitioners of transcendental meditation at Harvard Medical School in the early 1970's. They concluded that T.M. produces a profoundly relaxed state in the body while enhancing mental alertness. To learn more about this technique contact Dell Publishing at 1 Dag Hammerskjold Plaza New York, NY 10017 to obtain the book, <u>T.M. - Discovering Inner Energy and Overcoming Stress.</u>

I believe that your doctors prescribed medications, coupled with the exercises outlined and good common sense will accomplish the task of reducing and alleviating stress. Once stress has been removed the feelings of happiness and well being, will pervade your body and mind.

Chapter 6
STOP SMOKING NOW

A good plan today is better than a perfect plan tomorrow.
- Gen. George S. Patton.

All scientific research regarding cigarettes points to the fact that smoking causes cancer, emphysema, heart disease, premature aging and eventually death. Despite warnings printed on cigarette packs many people continue to puff happily along always thinking it will be the other guy that has a problem but not themselves.

Logically no one should smoke with all that has been learned about the risks of smoking. However, the habit roots itself quickly due to the fact that nicotine, like most addictive drugs, gets into the body and stays building up and storing its poison. The more we ingest the sooner our bodies develop a dependency for nicotine and smoking has proven to be as difficult a habit to break as heroin addiction.

The main ingredient needed to stop smoking is the real desire to quit on the part of the smoker himself. All the warnings in the world will not help unless the smoker has a very real desire to end his habit.

There are several types of smokers. The most prevalent of these is the person who uses cigarettes as a replacement for something missing in his or her life such as lack of self-esteem or love. This personality takes pleasure in the visual and oral effects of smoking. The smoker takes time to remove the cigarette from the pack, ignites his or her lighter, then the cigarette, slowly inhaling the hot fumes only to revel in watching the smoke itself upon exhaling. If this person were to smoke in the dark and be deprived of seeing the smoke he or she would miss more than 50% of the pleasure that they are used to.

The other type of personality uses identification with someone he looks up to such as a parent, the Marlborough Man or Humphrey Bogart, smoking in his movies. Remember how classy and sophisticated he looked while doing it; pulling the cigarette pack out of his pocket, lighting the match and taking those first few drags. Well, that look sure isn't worth dying for.   Like any other habit smoking can be replaced and you'll be so glad you took the slight effort needed.

In all the sessions of self-hypnosis along with the growing awareness of the bad taste and heat in your mouth and lungs, give yourself a vivid picture of how good it feels to breathe fresh air. Visualize yourself as a non-smoker and reinforce that with the ever-increasing feeling of well being.

Visualize from the beginning of each day that you will be feeling a clearing in your sinuses and your lungs, a new refreshingly clean taste in your mouth and all this will be accompanied by a gain in added vigor pulsing through your body.

See yourself enjoying being out in the fresh air and the exhilaration of conquering a very untidy and unhealthy habit. Your body and mind will now be in control of what you do, not the cigarettes. The cigarettes and nicotine will have lost their allure once you have begun to replace them with more positive habits that are things you choose to do rather than things you feel compelled to do.

There are a number of stop smoking aids available over the counter at your drug store. While these may help some people I highly recommend that you discuss this with your doctor. There are prescription drugs he may suggest for you and these should not be used while you are actually still smoking as they do contain nicotine. The addition of the nicotine in the medications plus the nicotine in the cigarettes could be very harmful. Use either plan but do yourself a great favor and stop smoking.

There is no substitute for the will to quit smoking. When you sincerely make the decision to be "smoke free," you will have accomplished half of the battle.

Regardless of any program you decide to use, the patch, Nicorette gum, prescription drugs, or the self-hypnosis method outlined, get started right away.

Because smoking happens to be not only a physical but a mental addiction as well, self-hypnosis should most definitely be employed to achieve lasting results.

Programming of the subconscious mind to stop smoking will only accelerate the good results you desire. Pride in any worthwhile accomplishment will enhance the feelings of happiness and satisfaction. Good health does promote happiness. Doesn't that sound worthwhile? The most important thing you need to do as simple as it may sound is to truly decide to quit.

Stop procrastinating!!! There is absolutely no doubt about the following statement. You have only two options; Live in good health by becoming a non-smoker or die from emphysema, asthma or cancer. It will be extremely painful and frightening.

Aversion therapy using hypnosis is affective. Visualize a cigarette attached to a diesel exhaust pipe on a semi truck. Smell and taste the hot emissions. These pictures will automatically bring to mind this disgusting connection.

See an ashtray filled with soggy cigarette butts. Imagine your face being forced into this revolting mess. Smell it, taste it and let yourself gag.

There is no beauty or charm in the aging and ugly discoloration of the face due to the use of tobacco. The hack and the wheeze are also unpleasant but Cancer and death are worse. This is hard but necessary love. Face the truth and change.

We have a wonderful tool to help our valid desire to quit smoking. It is the Tape recorder. Tape your own voice on the recorder using the following suggestions, and then play it back frequently. It does not require conscious effort to listen, just go about your daily life with these new truths about yourself being absorbed by the inner ear of the subconscious mind. This is a highly effective method called <u>Self Talk</u>. It works and works well. In the final chapter of this book on programming, I will go into more detail about this exciting method. Initially however, the basics of merely taping these, or your own suggestions and playing them back will be a great start. <u>Tape the following statements to your recorder and keep playing it back on a regular basis.</u>

I never smoke nor do I ever desire to.

I never short-change myself with narrow-minded beliefs. I allow myself to reach the broadest horizons of unlimited possibility.

I can do anything I believe I can do! Therefore, I do it. Every day I get better and better in every way.

I do not smoke. I enjoy breathing fresh air. I love filling my lungs with oxygen. I enjoy the aroma of flowers.

When I set goals I reach them. I know what I want to do with my life. I have a plan and it will succeed. I will succeed. I do not smoke.

I'm proud of who I am. I have total belief in myself and everything I do. I am proud to be a non-smoker. It makes me feel terrific.

Nothing ever holds me back. I am determined. Problems become advantages for me. I find possibilities in all things positive.

I have a tremendous abundance of energy—I feel very alive! I enjoy life. I keep myself looking ahead and liking it. The fact that I do not smoke tells me that I will be able to keep feeling this way for as long as I wish. I do not smoke.

I attain any goal I choose to pursue. Nothing stands in my way. I am a non-smoker. I do not smoke.

I do not fear anything or anyone. I have the strength, power, conviction, and confidence to overcome all obstacles. Smoking is not an obstacle as I do not smoke.

I love challenges and I meet them head on with a complete sense of power.

I am amazing. I have a clear picture in my mind of what I want. I see my goal as having already been accomplished. It's simple and I realize it. I know exactly what I want and I believe I will get it. Everything I do is up to me. I know I can do it too!

I am a winner. I am a non-smoker. I never smoke. I hate smoking. I hate the smell, the taste and the consequences.

Roadblocks never stay in my way. They are quickly removed as if they were never there at all. I am alive and growing stronger every day. I'm not going to stand still for anything. I do not smoke.

I always trust myself. I've got all that I need and I am fully aware of how to use it. I am utterly unstoppable. Anything I choose to do will be done. I harbor no doubt whatsoever. Just a simple as I know that I do not smoke, that I never smoke and that I never even desire to smoke. This is a great feeling. I am glad I can breathe easily.

I never allow myself excuses. I have the vitality to achieve more than ever before. I do not smoke.

I am a tremendously unique person. I believe in myself completely. I can do anything I want and avoid anything I do not want. I do not smoke. I love the smell of fresh air.

I have the uncanny power to live my dreams. I believe in them like I believe in myself. And that belief is so strong that there is nothing that diminishes my spirit.

I am practical and realistic, and I keep myself firmly grounded. I give freedom to my imagination.

I truly believe that with my individual fortress of faith, anything is possible.

If I have ever had any doubts about myself in the past, today is a good day to put them aside. I throw out any disbelief that ever held me back.

I know that I am headed in the right winning direction, and I look forward and never look back. I have the ability to focus on one thing at a time, so I concentrate my attention on the job at hand—and I get it done! I do not smoke.

Nothing can stand in my way. When I need extra determination, I have the power! When I need more energy and drive, it's all mine! I've got the power to get things done and I possess the patience to see it through, no matter what the challenge. I do not smoke. I breathe easily.

Being told "no" never bothers me. It increases my determination as well as my positive enthusiasm. I never smoke. I hate smoking. Smoking kills and I choose not to allow any power that is detrimental to me to overcome my new belief. I am truly a non-smoker and will remain that way the rest of my life. There is no doubt about this statement. I DO NOT SMOKE.

I love being a healthy non-smoker at all times and in all circumstances. I like myself and it shows. Being a non-smoker is easy for me. I was born that way and it is my nature to avoid harmful poisons. I do not worry. I am in control of my thinking. I think only those thoughts that create and fulfill the best in me.

I only focus on the positive, like the fact that I do not smoke and never wish to smoke. I enjoy fresh air and clear lungs. I feel terrific and each day I feel better and stronger.

All of my thoughts create healthy beliefs within me. My mind dwells only on those thoughts which create more harmony, perfect balance and well being within me and in the world around me. I automatically and always think in a decisive, power-filled and determined way. I am filled with resolution and absolute assurance of the best possible outcome in every thing I do and think. I always do everything I need to do when I need to do it. I never argue or let my emotions run against my desires. I do not smoke.

I enjoy being with the people I love, and because I do not smoke I can spend more time with them. I do not smoke.

My lungs and bronchials are strong, clear and healthy. I breathe deeply and fully. Taking care of my self physically is important to me. I like staying fit and feeling good. I do not smoke.

I am a non-smoker and proud of being so. I have a tremendous amount of energy and stamina. I never get tired. I love life and I'm glad to be alive.

I paint the world around me in the bright healthy light of optimism and self assurance of the best possible outcome of everything I say and do.

I do only those things that are the best for me to create the best within me, and therefore I do not smoke.

I never worry. I analyze and choose to create new and effective beliefs which will enhance my own ability to succeed.

I possess a multitude of excellent qualities. I have wonderful talents of which I am not yet fully aware. I continue to discover these new and hidden talents within me all the time. There is no limit. I am positive, I am confident, and I radiate good things.

I am bursting full of life. I am glad to be alive. I am a special person living at a special time. I feel good. I do not smoke.

I think happy and positive thoughts and my mind makes things right for me. I smile a lot and I laugh a lot and I am happy on the inside and the outside. I do not smoke.

Smoking disgusts me. I never smoke. Smokers do not breathe easily, but since I do not smoke, I do breathe easily.

Begin playing the tape you just made every day and night. It is extremely powerful and will surely work.

Use a substitute for smoking, such as chewing gum or sucking on a hard candy (sugar-free varieties for both are available in almost any grocery or convenience store).

In all the sessions of self-hypnosis along with the growing awareness of the bad taste and heat in your mouth and lungs, give yourself a vivid picture of how good it feels to breathe fresh air. Visualize yourself as a non-smoker and reinforce that with the ever-increasing feeling of well being. Visualize from the beginning of each day that you will be feeling a clearing in your sinuses and your lungs, a new refreshingly clean taste in your mouth and all this will be accompanied by a gain in added vigor pulsing through your body.

See yourself enjoying being out in the fresh air and enjoying the exhilaration of conquering a very untidy and unhealthy habit. Your body and mind will now be in control of what you do, not the cigarettes. The cigarettes and nicotine will have lost their allure once you have begun to replace them with more positive habits that are things you choose to do rather than things you feel compelled to do.

There are a number of stop smoking aids available over the counter at your drug store. While these may help some people I highly recommend that you discuss this with your doctor. There are prescription drugs he may suggest for you and these should not be used while you are actually still smoking as they do contain nicotine. The addition of the nicotine in the medications plus the nicotine in the cigarettes could be very harmful. Use either plan but do yourself a great favor and stop smoking now.

There is no substitute for the will to quit smoking. When you sincerely make the decision to be "smoke free," you will have accomplished half of the battle.

Regardless of any program you decide to use, the patch, Nicorette gum, prescription drugs, or the self-hypnosis and the Self Talk method outlined, get started right away.

Because smoking happens to be not only a physical but a mental addiction as well, self-hypnosis should most definitely be employed to achieve lasting results.

Programming of the subconscious mind to stop smoking will only accelerate the good results you desire. Pride in any worthwhile accomplishment will enhance the feelings of happiness and satisfaction. Good health does promote happiness. Doesn't that sound worthwhile? The most important thing you need to do as simple as it may sound is to truly _decide to quit_. Make the decision now to be nicotine free and get started today. You will be very happy that you did. Sometimes you have to go through hell to get to heaven but with this program it will be a short trip to freedom from the control of cigarettes and nicotine. Remember your two choices, a wonderful healthy life or an agonizing death. Choose well.

Chapter 7
I'M TOO DARN FAT

Reduce your plan to writing, the moment you complete this, you will have definitely given concrete form to the intangible desire.

- Napoleon Hill

In America today a vast number of people are overweight. This has opened a field for a multibillion-dollar industry in diet programs, "healthy" processed foods, and weight loss drugs. You've heard of most of them. Weight Watchers, Jenny Craig, Slim Fast and Lean Cuisine … are just a few of the many programs or products offered by this relatively new and extremely lucrative business.

People losing weight on these programs often regain the lost weight. These programs are missing the prime ingredient. The missing ingredient is total belief in a new self-image. You will lose weight but it will come back unless you completely change your self-image as you will always cooperate with what you believe about yourself.

Being overweight can prove to be an extremely serious risk to your health. I certainly approve of many of the well-known programs available.

U. C. L. A. Medical Center offers a great deal of free information concerning this subject available on the Internet. This is a valuable guide for advice on nutrition and weight control.

By law, the tobacco industry, for many years now has been required to post warning information regarding serious risks to your health on their products. The government overlooks the idea of printing warning labels on junk food knowing full well that most junk foods are packed with cholesterol. Heart disease, the number one killer in our country today, may be due in large part to the over consumption of foods laden with cholesterol and the cholesterol contained in junk foods is without a doubt as deadly to your health as the nicotine and tar in cigarettes.

Compulsive eating habits can be traced to a number of psychological reasons. I have found in my experience of over 20 years of helping people to lose weight that unhappiness generally stands out as the most powerful underlying cause of overeating.

The mechanics of losing weight are fairly simple. Eating the proper foods, reducing the amount of caloric intake and ridding the body of excess fat through exercise, are all necessary requirements for losing weight. I have worked with doctors and dietitians on this program and I strongly urge you to consult your physician before undertaking any diet plan.

It is easy to understand the frustration of dieters. They would like to find the magic cure, one that would require no effort on their part but unfortunately, it does not work that way. A specific plan must be followed and adhered to religiously to accomplish the result desired. We must practice patience and be focused with a determination to succeed.

A safe amount of weight to lose ranges approximately from three to four pounds a week, which will not sap your energy in the slightest. Three pounds of weight reduction per week translates to twelve pounds of weight loss per month. In four months you will have rid yourself of forty-eight pounds of unwanted fat. Remember that you didn't go to bed slender one night then wake up in the morning with an obesity problem. It took a lot of digesting to become overweight so don't expect a miracle cure.

You can insure your success with very little discomfort. You will find this a very enjoyable and rewarding plan to follow. The answer to permanent, safe weight reduction lies in the most powerful part of your brain, the subconscious mind. We begin by reprogramming the subconscious mind to truly believe that you are now already at your desired weight. Whatever you sincerely believe in your subconscious mind constitutes a blueprint for your life that you will always cooperate with. Many overweight people have a strong belief in their inner consciousness that they are now and always will be obese. This inner belief is so powerful that it becomes a self-fulfilling prophecy.

As you begin to lose pounds and inches through dieting there remains an inner discomfort because what is occurring is contrary to what your subconscious mind has been programmed to believe about yourself.

Your reasoning mind desires that you lose weight in order to look better and improve your health. These contradictory thoughts in your mind cause a conflict resulting in stress and unhappiness.

In order to achieve success both the conscious and subconscious mind must act in harmony. For this reason it becomes totally necessary to reprogram this previously held inner belief. That is why we instill into the subconscious mind a belief that your desired appearance has already been accomplished. This new belief about yourself must override the former negative picture with which you have cooperated for such a long time.

Through the visualization process you will gradually construct a new blueprint in this most powerful part of your brain. Your mind, now totally integrated and focused on the way you wish to be, will guide you rapidly to the realization of your goal. The complete acceptance and belief regarding the new you is the positive blueprint you will now follow.

It is synchronized to work in unison to guide you to success.

As soon as the subconscious mind really accepts that you are actually the way you wish to become you will automatically and happily do all the things needed to cooperate with that new belief. This makes it almost effortless to reach your desired goal.

The marvelous part about this program is that it bases itself on the fact that you won't need to consciously force yourself to diet or exercise. All these things will actually become fun, satisfying and extremely easy. The very powerful subconscious mind acts just like a guided missile aimed at your goal. When you have the right target selected, you will be well on your way to reaching the results you consciously desire. Although it requires repetition you will find these exercises soothing and refreshing.

Within a few short weeks you will notice your eating habits changing for the better. You will feel younger and far more vital. You will look great and others will be delighted with the changes in you.

You will be using self-hypnosis, powerful visualization and true belief in the end result. The byproducts will be a new confidence, greater pride, much lower feelings of stress and the development of a happy, sparkling, personality to share with your family and friends.

Visualization Program

Use the self-hypnosis technique and get to a deep but comfortably relaxed state. The first step in your mind should be to design a private room that no one can enter except you. This will be your sanctuary for programming your inner mind. Decide on the size of the room you like and color the walls and ceiling in the most pleasing way for you. Carpet the floor anyway you find most pleasant. Feel the texture of the carpet and walls and even smell the newness of it all. Now take your time to create and arrange the furniture and pictures. Make all of these things beautiful and restful.

Once these things are done you have created your inner retreat where you will begin to change your life for the better. Relax in one of the chairs and listen to soft music from your stereo. Become as familiar with this new room as you possibly can. After you have finished this task and rested for a time in this new environment you notice that at both ends of the room are ceiling to floor and wall-to-wall mirrors.

Go to the first mirror and look at your reflection. You see yourself as you are in appearance right now and don't pull any punches. Look at your complexion, facial expression and posture. Be acutely aware of your overweight condition and the sad, unhappy face in the mirror. Be brutally honest with yourself. You find this reflection displeasing to you.

Now go to the mirror at the opposite end of the room and look at your reflection in this, the "Inner Reality Mirror." See yourself in this mirror just the way you want to become. Notice that the excess weight no longer exists. Your body looks just the way you want it to be.

You are perfectly formed and at your desired weight and appearance. Your complexion glows, you are happy and smiling. With your posture erect the texture and coloring of your skin perfect; you now look happy, young, and vital.

The person you see before you in the glass will be you just the way you want to be and will allow you to be just as happy as you want to feel and you're making it happen right now! Your visualization stems from the way you really are inside and very soon it will be you on the outside as well.

Now command the first mirror to vanish. Look back and see that it is gone, never to return. Now you can relax and enjoy the new you. Bask in this sensation. Make it real and make it very vivid.

Relax in your secret room and feel delighted with yourself. Each time you return to this imagined room, the belief in the changes you wish for become stronger and more real.   Spend as much time as you can here and keep looking at the new you in the "Inner Reality Mirror."

In order to strengthen this imagery see yourself in the inner reality mirror changing into different clothing, admiring the way the different outfits become you. Pose in various positions and observe your reflection closely. See yourself performing mild exercises and continually promote the feeling of happiness and confidence. Change your hairstyle if you wish and even change the color of your makeup.

Do anything you can think of to make these visualizations become more vivid and real. Involve all your five senses during this experience. You are sending very powerful programming messages to your subconscious mind in order to replace the old negative beliefs regarding yourself with a new and positive belief that will cause the happy changes you desire to become reality.

Throughout this book I will constantly remind you that your subconscious mind is unable to recognize the difference between a real event and an event that is vividly imagined. That is why this visualization exercise must be made to seem as real as possible. Soon the subconscious mind will accept these suggestions as reality and bring about all the changes needed for you to become the person you wish to be.

When ending the session tell yourself that each and every time you practice this visualization it will become more real and vivid until you truly believe this with all your heart, mind and soul.

Using the self-hypnosis program count yourself up, 0-1-2-3-4-5- Wide Awake, Wide Awake. You will wake up feeling happy, rested and confident. You will sleep peacefully at night, and awaken in the morning feeling refreshed and filled with energy.

Reinforce this during the day by using positive, affirmative notes and pictures, referring to them often, and saying to yourself, "THIS IS ME RIGHT NOW!"

As your subconscious mind begins to truly believe this it will prompt you to do all of the things necessary to cooperate with this new self-image.

Dieting and exercise will become enjoyable. Overeating will become a thing of the past. You will begin to shed pounds and inches within the first week. Other people will begin to notice this outward change and so will you. Practice these sessions daily and you will never be disappointed for putting in the effort required. Repetition is paramount in order for good habits to be formed and bad habits will be left by the wayside.

One of the first feelings you will find yourself aware of when you begin practicing the exercises will be a happy inner-glow. The real you has been trapped inside an overweight body. The feeling of release from this unpleasant appearance will manifest itself daily.

As you envision yourself as you wish to become, you will begin to realize the attractiveness of your true self. The real you is just waiting for release from a prison of obesity.

You have envisioned what the real you looks like in the Inner Reality Mirror. Every week that passes will bring you closer to your ultimate goal. The real you feels happy and confident as you begin to shed pounds and inches. The belief you have programmed into your mind becomes stronger every day.

You will experience a new freedom starting from within and most surely that will be reflected in your outer appearance. Feelings of joy and true happiness begin growing in power with each day that passes. You are setting yourself free. You are breaking the chains of habit and gaining control of a life that you can be very proud of, your own. As you progress in your daily sessions you start improving your confidence and belief in a trim, healthy, sound body. Persist in the program. Soon the results will be very evident. You will bask in the emotions of happiness and pride.

You may find yourself gazing in the mirror and saying, "Hey, I look pretty darn good." A definite, noticeably perceivable difference will reveal itself and when it does, you will have the benefit of reaping all the rewards it will bring.

Chapter 8
DESENSITIZING PHOBIAS

Fear is that little dark room where negatives are developed.

- Michael Pritchard.

The majority of people are able to keep their fears in proper perspective. They do not have severe reactions to fears and phobias so these play a very minor part in their lives. Some people have phobias regarding things such as spiders, snakes and mice. Others fear thunderstorms, enclosed places, flying, being alone or being in the dark.

When a person has a limited number of such phobias their likelihood of over sensitizing their nervous system is very slight. In this type of individual phobias are quickly and easily eradicated. Seeing their fear from a reasoning point of view often defuses the phobia. Discussing the fear openly with your physician helps you realize just how silly that fear is. It would be a good idea to use a tape recorder during such a discussion and play the recording back to yourself to reinforce your understanding of how small an influence the phobia has in your life.

Phobias are generally irrational fears of things or situations that truly pose no real physical danger to us.

Generally speaking, facing the fear directly conquers fear. Allow it to do its worst. The visualization process is a convenient way of beginning this training for elimination of the phobia.

Many people suffer from phobias, which vary in degree and intensity. These phobias are usually associated with a place or a situation. If you feel very uncomfortable speaking in front of a group, attending a party or just stuck in traffic, a method exists to dramatically decrease and often entirely remove that anxiety.

Basically the symptoms of the anxiety are so unpleasant to tolerate that we are willing to do almost anything possible to avoid these symptoms.

We also tend to associate the symptoms with the place or situation where we seem to experience them. These are just symptoms caused by fear and are a normal neurological response to fear. Rapid heartbeat, increased blood pressure, flushing of the skin, palpitations, gasping for air etc., are the primitive mind's way of preparing our bodies for fight or flight. We are all geared up to take action but often we fail to find an appropriate action to deal with how we feel. We cannot, for instance, physically assault an audience if we are feeling stressed as a speaker or performer and we would look extremely foolish if we charged off the stage and out of the door.

The symptoms, however, are so unpleasant that we just avoid getting ourselves into a situation that we believe will trigger these feelings. Avoidance of more and more of these situations and places severely limits our ability to lead a happy life and experience the success we would like to have.

The original causes for the feelings of fear really serve little purpose in discovering. Toning down and eradicating the fear will be the way to experience more happiness and enjoyment in life. It does seem that every time we experience these bodily symptoms they seem to become stronger and more fear provoking.

While understanding that these physiological changes are normal we must realize that in many fearful situations we are reacting to a perceived danger yet in truth, the danger we perceive poses no real physical threat to us at all. If you were faced with a loose, angry lion, these symptoms though unpleasant, would prepare you to save your life by releasing in you far greater strength and speed for coping this very real physical danger. Even if the bodily changes in you were to freeze you into immobility, providing you with the appearance of death, that response might also save your life.

The flow of adrenaline in your body, which causes the symptoms, is controlled by your sympathetic nervous system and that system has been prompted into activity by the perception of danger, real or imagined, in your mind.

It therefore proves necessary to alter these conscious perceptions and defuse the false impressions that have caused the undue anxiety.

To accomplish this task use the self-hypnosis technique to enter a very deeply relaxed state of visualization and imagination. When you have achieved deep relaxation in your body and mind, confront the weakest of the phobias first. In this hypnotic state imagine yourself in the place or situation that normally triggers that particular anxiety. From force of habit you will begin to experience the anxiety again but at the same time you are aware that your body is deeply relaxed.

Now focus your attention on the deeper relaxation of the body while abandoning the fear-provoking situation you were imagining. When you have again become comfortably relaxed turn your attention back to the place or situation that triggered the fear. When anxiety begins to return it will be less powerful. Again place total attention on relaxation in your body and forget the imagery that prompted the discomfort.

After a short time, return to the old situation that caused the anxiety, remembering that you are in a very relaxed state and continually deepening within that state while noting also that the anxiety has greatly diminished. Leave that situation again and focus on your calm, relaxed feeling until you are totally at ease.

This process must be repeated over and over again until you feel less and less anxiety as you face the visualization. Soon you will begin to feel like yawning or smiling. This is a very good indication that the triggering situation that you have been working on has been defused. You will know when this is accomplished when you place yourself in the situation again mentally. You will have no anxiety whatever. In this exercise familiarity does breed contempt towards the thing that prompted your discomfort in the past.

You have mastered the technique of defusing the weakest of the triggering situations. With this knowledge and confidence you can proceed in succeeding sessions to defuse the rest one at a time. Keep at this diligently and you will be amazed at how soon you will be in comfortable control of yourself and the way you will be able to feel at ease in your environment.

I always recommend that you have a complete physical examination by a doctor to be sure that there is no physical condition that causes the symptoms.

Shortages of certain vitamins can contribute to nervousness. Hypoglycemia also produces symptoms that are similar to anxiety. A good doctor may recommend a mild tranquilizer to be taken over a short period of time. This medication used in conjunction with the defusing technique described will be of benefit.

As you progress in relaxation techniques you will soon be able to face the triggering situations in reality.

Although these experiences may prompt some degree of anxiety they will, by practicing them through repetition, reduce and ultimately eliminate the anxieties you felt when actually faced with the real experience or cause of the anxious reaction.

One should then face the fear provoking circumstance in a real situation, and by learning to accept the fear response for what it is; a normal biological reaction of the body, gradually defuse that fear entirely.

We possess two kinds of fears. The first is our conscious perception of a perceived danger and the second is a fear of our own symptoms produced by a flood of adrenaline, which causes unpleasant feelings in our body. If you are able to avoid having the first fear by defusing it completely then the second fear will not occur. Facing a fear will weaken it but avoiding the fear-producing situation gives it more strength. Soon, the real experience will cease to affect you. This program will build up your confidence and self-esteem. The result will be a feeling of pride and self-confidence.

There is also a treatment called, "Paradoxical Intention."

Since we do not have voluntary control over our autonomic nervous system we my experience feelings of dizziness, heart palpitations, panic etc. The "Paradoxical Intention" program was developed to help us deal with autonomic nervous system and has proven to be quite successful.

In this treatment the patient is encouraged to intentionally try to produce a panic attack or dizziness or blushing. The patient is unable to make these things happen. By trying to produce these symptoms and being unable to make them occur the patient will be developing an attitude of becoming unafraid of the symptoms. Often he will feel silly about the symptoms and start laughing about this paradox. In effect he puts distance between himself and the fear of the symptoms. This removal of the fear will actually overcome the symptom entirely. This treatment should be used under the direction of a qualified psychiatrist that is familiar with the techniques developed by Dr. Victor Frankl.

<u>Agoraphobia</u>

"In the case of Agoraphobia the patient's nervous system has become so highly sensitized that a common response is a panic attack. Even when an Agoraphobic patient becomes fully aware of the mechanics of the chemical causes of the panic attack he/she fears the unpleasant symptoms so much that the normal desensitizing program and psychotherapy do little to alleviate this condition. The Agoraphobic retreats from situations that seem associated with the panic attacks.

The recommended treatment is drug therapy combined with counseling and desensitization methods. This condition is far more severe than common phobias and a doctor who is well versed in this field should treat the patient.

Psychotherapy alone will not help the problem of a severe case of Agoraphobia, as the patient is more afraid of the symptoms than by people, places or things. It is possible that this condition may be entirely due to a chemical imbalance in the patient's brain.

For most people with relatively minor phobias the simple desensitizing program I describe in this chapter will be very efficient and successful. Once mastered, happiness will find its place in your life again. Remember, you can do whatever you choose if you want to badly enough.

Chapter 9
BECOME YOUNG NOW

*Youth is happy because it has the ability to see beauty.
Anyone, who keeps the ability to see beauty, never grows
old.*

- Franz Kafka.

The old saying, "Age is Just a Number," has some real validity. There are many older people who not only behave young but also look and act many years younger than their chronological age. You have probably seen very young people that look and act much older than they really are.

Age serves not just a physical state but a mental state as well. When we think and act younger than we are we usually look and feel far younger. The scientific community has studied the aging process for a great number of years without much success in understanding the process.

Everyone would like to bathe in the fountain of youth. Just look at all the creams and lotions that the American public buys and uses each day.

Naturally, as we grow older, there are physical changes that take place in our bodies. Decrease in scalp foliage, wrinkles, poorer vision etc., seem to affect us all. The old Burma Shave sign comes to mind, "In this vale of toil and sin, our head grows bald, but not our chin." Depending on our genes, some of us retain a lot of hair on our heads, as we get older. Many people seem to get fewer wrinkles than others. The one truism that applies to most of us is that we still feel like we are in our twenties, at least mentally.

The more active physically and mentally a person is, the younger they appear, feel, and behave. Staying interested in what goes on around us is a great tonic for staying young.

Mild physical exercise on a daily basis will keep our bodies in better condition.

Taking care of medical problems as they arise is also an important factor. Proper diet is very necessary as being overweight puts a tremendous stress on the body. Smoking is proven to be a major contributing factor to premature aging. Some researchers are testing HGH (Human Growth Hormone) with exciting results. Studies have shown that the use of HGH indicates a slowing down of the aging process and perhaps a reversal of some aging as well. As we grow older chronologically, aging is accompanied by a decrease in the body's hormonal output. A hormone called *SOMATOTROPIN* begins to decline rapidly at the age of thirty onward. This decline seems to cause a disruption of the entire hormonal system.

Many wealthy people were traveling to Europe to take a series of very expensive injections of HGH with great results. It is possible to obtain HGH in tablet form or in oral spray, which is now available in The United States. This makes HGH inexpensive and easy to use. According to an article by Daniel Rudman M.D. in The New England Journal of Medicine, he states, *"The overall deterioration of the body that comes with growing old is not inevitable…. We now realize that some aspects of it can be prevented or reversed."* Science marches on and we may see some major breakthroughs in the near future.

The best time for preparing to remain young is when we are already chronologically young. Exercise, proper diet and mental discipline practiced at a young age, will most certainly help keep us looking and feeling young for a much greater period of time.

Preconceived notions about growing old will have a definite affect on the aging process. We are led to believe early in life that by age fifty we are over the hill and beginning to dodder. If we expect to be old at age fifty our expectations will probably be fulfilled. Belief plays such a powerful role in our lives and I can never stress enough how much it affects the way we look, feel and behave. The way you believe, in that inner mind, is the way you will be.

If you enjoy being around younger people the chances are that you will feel younger than the ones who only socialize with people of their own age group. Being interested and involved in the music and thinking of younger people will have a strong influence on your apparent age.

My own son was a singer in a contemporary rock band. Ten years ago I hated loud rock music, but after being exposed to countless practices and stage shows, I actually found myself getting involved and I actually came to enjoy that type of music. I haven't given up the pleasure of listening to the big bands, blues, opera and country western, but I have also added a different kind of musical expression to the sounds I enjoy hearing. People with an open mind can also truly enjoy Rock and Roll.

Young people respond well to older folks who take an active part by understanding and appreciating the more current trends. Physically acting young and thinking young and interacting with younger people will cause you to look and feel younger. You may not be as foxy as you used to be but if you will change your innermost belief to one in which you feel and act young you will add a zest and sparkle to your personality and appearance.

Doing things that are fun, like walking on the beach, going fishing, playing golf or tennis, dancing and so on, will actually increase your physical vitality. Things we find fun to do keep us young in mind and body. If you are unable to be physically active try to find other hobbies or outlets that will allow you to express your youthful inner side.

Let it out. Expose all of your exuberance and share it with others. Find activities that you can be truly interested in and learn to enjoy. Learn to love life and to love people. Never let yourself become bored.

Exposing your mind to new experiences is a wonderful way to improve your attitude toward living. Something exciting or challenging awaits you and all you need to do, very simply is, decide to do it and then put it into practice. Be free and give yourself a new lease on a youthful life.

Happiness is yours for the taking at any age. The more you smile, the more you laugh and the more active and interested you are in the life that surrounds you, the more you will feel and look younger.

Stagnating assures you will grow old before your time. The old saying is, "When you're green you grow, when you're ripe you rot." Please, do not let yourself rot. Every person can change if they decide to and though some changes are painful this one will offer you a youthful feeling that should be painless. Please take some of these suggestions and practice them. If you smoke, quit. If you're overweight, diet and get in shape. If you're bored, find an activity that wakes you up to a happy life. Whatever makes you unhappy in life needs to be addressed. Focusing on the solution to the problem rather than dwelling on the problem itself will even bring satisfaction due to the fact you know that you are making a sincere effort to face the problem and ultimately overcome it.

The practice of self-hypnosis to program your inner mind to believe you are younger, fitter, and more active, will be of great benefit. Use it in your daily routine to reinforce the conscious thoughts you wish to have and the actions you need take while starting on your journey into creating the youthful inner you. As each day passes you will begin to notice that the, "flowers smell sweeter, and your food tastes better." You will begin feeling younger and more vital. Just believe it and behave in that way. Positive results are sure to follow.

Happiness is contagious; spread it around all you can. It will come back to you in abundance. People love to associate with happy, smiling people. Be one of those smiling people. We all have a lot to offer other people. Give of yourself. Allow others to come into your space. Sometimes you may be vulnerable but that just allows others to share your own human nature with theirs.

Enjoy every day you live. Enjoy everyone you meet. Look forward to every challenge that comes along with confidence and joy. Smile all you can and watch the world respond to you with more happiness than you ever thought anyone could receive.

"Sadness shared is halved. Happiness shared is doubled."
- Anonymous.

Chapter 10
CAN YOU BE HAPPILY MARRIED?

Marriage has many pains, but celibacy has no pleasures.
- Samuel Johnson.

Approximately forty percent of current marriages end in divorce. Conversely new marriages are expected to rise by sixty five percent over the next two years.

People marry for a great number of different reasons. Unfortunately some of the motivations are rather self-seeking, frivolous and immature. Looking for security in marriage proves rather childish as circumstances are always changing and security can be swept away in a moment.

Romance is one of the more ambiguous motives for marriage. Sentimental novels and movies have promoted romance for many years now. The desire for an attractive sex partner in marriage certainly can well be understood but as a primary motive for marriage, it provides a weak basis for a sound and lasting union. Whatever the reason, people will continue to marry and many will be successful at achieving a happy and lasting relationship. I believe that to have a truly happy marriage both partners should be emotionally mature and be very close friends as well.

Their friendship should be one in which each desires the ultimate happiness for the other. This creates a bond that will be difficult to break.

A decline in morality in our country really opens up a big can of worms. Many spouses are inclined to believe that the grass grows greener on the other side of the fence. Attraction to the opposite sex is normal, but those who cross the line to infidelity, will regret doing that for the rest of their lives. Flirting when at parties or in bars, while commonplace, can lead to very unfortunate consequences.

The movies, television shows and magazines play down extramarital affairs as just normal behavior. When infidelity has occurred the offended party may be hurt so deeply that their whole outlook on life may be ruined. They may find it in their hearts to forgive but they will never be able to get rid of the memory of the betrayal. That memory can poison their trust and their happiness. It is only human to wish to escape from a painful situation and it takes great courage and understanding to love and persevere in that union. Many people stay together for the sake of their children or for financial security. Sometimes they remain together out of fear of facing the outside world alone. Happiness in this situation is out of the question. Another solution must be sought. If there exists something worth saving maybe the partners can explore their personalities and feelings more closely, offering sincere acceptance of each other's faults, to find the love that once brought them together.

Before committing oneself to marriage I believe that several very important criteria should be met.

You should be very close friends with each other whether or not you go into marriage. A true and completely understanding friendship is the best foundation for happiness in marriage. Close friends enjoy each other's company and are less likely to do or say things that might harm their friendship. Developing the ability to understand the way your friend talks and acts eliminates misunderstandings before they become serious. You develop a feeling of comfort just being with each other. This closeness will help create and maintain a happy atmosphere in which to live.

You should share the same interests and opinions. By sharing most of the same opinions and social interests there is less apt to be any personality clashes. You will disagree on many things and each person will probably have a pet activity they enjoy that the other partner does not care to share. This is good, as everyone needs some personal time away from his or her spouse. Giving each other private time and freedom makes the time spent together far more rewarding. You must have open and clear communication with one another and share your deepest secrets, even if it means taking a great risk. Open communication and understanding are as necessary in a marriage as they are in the operation of a business.

Talking together each day clarifies plans, feelings, timing and financial concerns. It is wise to share in the setting of priorities in regard to the education of children, living location, employment concerns and even entertainment. This eliminates confusion over what actions should be taken and as well as the timing for these actions.

It is important to discuss personal emotional feelings. This provides the opportunity to defuse any false notions, which could otherwise grow into uncomfortable sensitivities and hard feelings.

The reasons for your desire to marry should be honestly understood and agreed to with each other. These should be openly shared because unless you agree on the true, rational basis for getting married, it may later lead to an unhappy result. If each partner is expecting something else trouble will certainly come. If both partners are agreed on the same reason for marriage the chances for success are greatly improved.

There should be a physical, emotional and intellectual attraction for each other. The best marriage partners almost automatically have a strong physical and emotional attraction for one another. It is a real blessing if they share in the same intellectual pursuits. This bonds them more closely together and adds spice to their relationship. There must be a clear-cut goal in your minds for the purpose of uniting, such as a home, children, companionship, mutual respect and trust.

Having the same goals in marriage helps mates work together through the difficult times that we all experience. This mutual commitment keeps us focused and in harmony. Side issues lose their power to interfere with our combined determination to succeed.

Finally, there must be total commitment, regardless of any hardships that may arise in the future. Without the total commitment to the success of the marriage by both partners there is only a slight chance of true happiness. Unless you are both completely committed to one another you should call a halt to the proposed union and start looking for someone else to share your life.

One of the biggest problems before and after marriage is communication. Unfortunately, many people do not truly understand what the other person is saying and meaning.

Thanks to Dr. John Kappas and his colleagues at the Hypnosis Motivation Institute in Tarzana, California, we now have a clearer way to understand one another. In a great psychological breakthrough he discovered that in early youth people developed different ways of understanding others and of expressing themselves.

One of the conditions of communication, he termed, physical *suggestibility*. This personality is one who takes in information literally but expresses his thoughts inferentially.

The person with this type of learned behavior has a problem in communicating with a person who speaks and understands from the same paradigm. The personality, who understands through *inference* is termed an *emotional suggestible*.

People that have an *emotional-suggestible* personality express information literally. Basically, these terms refer to the way that person learned how to learn and understand communication in early youth. This suggests why opposites seem to attract one another. Since the physical suggestible personality speaks through inference, and that is exactly the way the emotional suggestible person understands the information being conveyed, they are able to communicate. Conversely, the emotional suggestible person is relaying information literally, which is the way the physical suggestible person understands.

The problem in communication arises when a physical suggestible person converses with another predominately physical suggestible, as the information is given inferentially to a person who only understands literally. The same problem occurs when an emotional suggestible person tries to communicate with another emotional suggestible personality. It is a matter of not being able to clearly understand what the other is saying. Unless this barrier to understand and communicate honestly and accurately can be removed or truly adapted to problems and unhappiness will surely occur.

The family unit truly signifies the backbone of our society and as such, marriage should never be taken lightly. Love is a very misunderstood word and concept. Love should be a feeling of unconditional caring for the object of ones devotion and affection. Actions must outwardly show the very deep and personal commitment of each married partner towards the other. Both must share that same unconditional and total commitment.

Many churches now are conducting programs of premarital instruction. These programs demonstrate a no nonsense approach to marriage. You have the time to explore each other's feelings, beliefs and desires. In this way you will soon know if you will get along well with each other and realize the duties and responsibilities of marriage. Avail yourself of the counseling offered. Hopefully you will exercise the self-control not to leap into a marriage that might be doomed to failure. Make sure you are right for each other. The pain of divorce can prove devastating. We all have divorced friends and many of them carry around negative excess baggage from the way things turned out. The offended party will have a tendency to become bitter towards the opposite sex usually projecting the bad traits of the ex-spouse on others who actually are not inclined to have these undesirable characteristics.

When contemplating marriage or even in attempting to save a marriage headed toward the rocks, professional help should be sought from a priest, minister, Rabbi or marriage counselor.

Get some advice on things you can do or should do before making any drastic decisions. It might confirm your beliefs, or you may be dissuaded from doing something that you might eventually regret.

Using self-hypnosis, you can achieve a relaxed and unemotional state and then permit your subconscious mind to gather the data and devise a reasonable plan for dealing with the problems and questions involved, especially prior to marriage. The inner mind will prompt you to do all the things needed to come to a rational and sane plan for a wise marriage decision. Some marital problems are very severe and outside help must be sought.

Physical and mental abuse in a marriage can become more than unpleasant. Sometimes this problem is life threatening. In this marital situation you should consider divorce and legal protection. This is certainly true when it involves battered wives or child abuse. This dangerous behavior indicates that a form of insanity exists. This type of irrational conduct is being exposed more frequently in the media.

Some women, out of fear, refuse to testify against their spouses and remain in their futile marriages. The legal system must be used when dealing with this severe problem.

No one should feel compelled to live in such frightening circumstances.

There are programs in many cities to assist women and children existing in such a terrible home environment but a need for an increase in penalties for child abuse and spousal abuse should and must be realized. Hopefully, some legislators will pay more attention to the welfare of these victims.

Many churches and civic groups have become involved in assisting these unfortunate people, working closely with shelters and law enforcement agencies.

Ultimately the wives in these situations need to take the initiative and contact the agencies that have the power to give them advice, protection and aid. Get out of this miserable situation as soon as possible. You will be able to adjust to a new life, without fear, and be far happier than you are now. You should definitely consult a doctor, counselor and religious leader for advice and assistance.

Chapter 11
YOU MAKE ME CRANKY

The really happy person is the one who can enjoy the scenery, even when they have to take a detour.
- Sir James Jeans

One of the stumbling blocks to being happy is the habit of holding a grudge against someone else. The feeling of being treated unfairly by others and the desire to get even with them illustrates a habit that causes a great deal of unhappiness and wasted energy. If you are this type of person, the one who always wants the books to be balanced in relationship to others, you had better do some logical thinking about the cost of this negative trait to you.

Be totally honest with yourself, then you will understand that the person, who offended you often times may not even be aware that he has given any offense. That person expends no energy stewing about the very thing that you are allowing yourself to feel unnecessary grief over.

We are only human and cannot know exactly what another person thinks or feels. Most people are not malicious and do not put much thought behind their unkind action or remark.

The person who truly suffers in the situation mentioned here is the one who dwells on the real or supposed offenses toward their own person.

We are all by nature looking out for our own good and ourselves. On the other hand we often expect the opposite behavior from others. We want others to hold us in high esteem and treat us with the utmost deference. We need to behave toward others, as we would like them to behave toward us. This positive activity will offer no guarantees that other people will respond the same way but you will feel better and the majority of people will react in a positive way.

We have no direct way of controlling the comments and behavior of other people. The people we enjoy being around are the ones who show a genuine concern for our own personal welfare and happiness. When we look for these personality traits in our friends and relatives we are bound to be disappointed. They have their own lives to lead and their own welfare to be concerned with.

If we take stock of our personal attitude towards other people we discover that we do not really take a deep personal interest in how they feel or what they think. Human nature compels us to understand people and affairs insofar as they affect us personally. We all tend to expect people to behave the way it suits us and seem to be amazed when they don't conform to what in our mind seems to be the only just response or course to take.

When someone has been rather abrupt with us and hurt our feelings, it usually had nothing to do with us personally; rather they had some pressing worry or obligation that just didn't allow them the time to spend on our desire to talk with them.

In fact, in this busy life we lead, people are torn between conflicting duties and decisions. We should be grateful that they did not spend that time dumping all their problems on our ears. We have all experienced supposed rebuffs from another only to find out later that person had just undergone a traumatic experience in their own life and didn't tell us what their problem was.

Recognize the fact that we cannot change other people to suit us but that we can change ourselves and our attitudes toward others.

When we take a close scrutiny of our own traits we will more than likely discover that the traits we dislike in others are usually the same traits inherent within ourselves.

In order to become a truly happy person we must learn to be tolerant and forgiving. When we have reached a state of being by nature more tolerant and forgiving, we will have removed one of the prime causes of unhappiness in our lives. The ability to be happy lies inside us all.

In the business world a salesperson must learn to accept rejection without taking it personally. The old saying is that the best salespeople in the world have the skin of a rhinoceros. They refuse to allow rejection to affect their inner being or ego. They put on a great big smile and greet their next prospect with a happy, confident attitude. When rejections are not taken as a personal affront, they have very little influence on our self-esteem and therefore do not make us feel unhappy. This should be true in our daily intercourse with other people.

When things are written down on paper it makes them much easier for our minds to analyze. I suggest you make a list of the things others do that irritate you. Directly beneath each statement honestly write down if you are guilty of these same failings and also the degree in which you tend to practice these negative traits.

Examples

OTHERS: She always seems to hog the conversation.
ME: I talk about me almost all the time.
OTHERS: He never seems to listen to a word I say.
ME: I can't wait for him to shut up so I can say what I feel.
OTHERS: He's always too busy to help.
ME: I've got my own problems to take care of. I can't spare the time to help him.
OTHERS: She just doesn't share my political views.

ME: My views are more important than hers.
OTHERS: He always thinks he's right about every-
   thing.
ME: I think I'm always right about everything.
OTHERS: She is so set in her ways, what a closed mind
   she has.
ME: Am I really that set in my ways?

This list could go on forever but the real reason for listing these habits is to make a true self-examination. We are creatures of habit and bad habits can be replaced with good ones. What we do not like in others we usually find as dominant personality traits in our own behavior. When we recognize this fact we must come to a decision. Since we cannot change the other person, are we willing in order to be happy to change ourselves?

The first step to take in this course is forgiveness. We must learn to recognize that we do have failings and be able to forgive ourselves for our own very human weaknesses.

This means to really forgive ourselves for our own mistakes and make a decision to change them for the better. Once we are able to recognize the faults in ourselves and forgive our weakness we are then in a position to understand and forgive others.

When we are able to develop into the kind of person we like to be around it will in time have a positive influence on the people we come in contact with. The awareness of these faults in ourselves puts us in the position of being able to tolerate those faults in others.

As we learn to tolerate the other person we also become able to understand and forgive them as well.

When we truly forgive others we remove the reason for being unhappy due to an influence outside ourselves that we have been guilty of as well.

True forgiveness can prove to be a difficult process. Hitting back or holding a grudge offers nothing but negative feelings and pain. What good does that accomplish? Realize that hatred and anger held inside is much like sewer gas that builds up and this pent up hatred causes us to feel miserable.

Maybe the person who offended you is no longer involved in your life. Maybe the person you hate or hold a grudge against has already died but you still feel the anger. Possibly the person you need to forgive might be someone with whom you are in constant contact.

Whatever the situation, be aware that by forgiving them you are actually freeing yourself from a condition that affects you adversely both physically and psychologically. I am not suggesting that you become a doormat to be walked over.

Do not continue to take abuse from anyone but realize that when you truly forgive him or her you are freeing yourself from a very unhealthy condition that causes you to feel unhappy. Whether the people involved that hurt you are still in your life or have moved away or died, this formula will free you from the pain and anger you have harbored.

Read the following exercise and commit it to memory, then do the exercise as many times as it takes to give you the assurance that you have successfully achieved the state of true forgiveness.

Exercise

While seated, place your hands, palms down, on your thighs. Closing your eyes, recall the person and event that hurt or offended you; bringing the memory back in vivid detail. As you do this, clench your fist. You will notice that as you go deeper into the recollection your fist will get tighter and tighter. Your fist signifies the grip with which you are holding onto your anger. Try to visualize that your fist has actually closed tightly over the event and its feelings. Next, visualize that person as someone in great pain and when you finally decide to let go and forgive you will be eliminating that pain.

Slowly, very slowly, allow your fist to unclench and in your mind keep repeating I forgive you, I forgive you. I no longer hang onto anger and hate. As your hand continues to open you begin to feel a peaceful release of the pent up emotions. As your hand relaxes and opens entirely, palm up, you will feel a wonderful sense of relief both physically and mentally and the hurt and anger no longer exist.

You may need to practice this exercise several times before you have achieved true forgiveness. Whatever it takes it is most necessary to reach this state in order to rid yourself of conflict and allow yourself to be truly happy.

An unforgiving nature leads to, or stems from, an unhappy nature. If we want to lead a happy life we will learn to practice tolerance and forgiveness toward ourselves and towards everyone we meet. No one truly wants to be miserable or unhappy. Some people just do not realize what physical and psychological effects their inability to forgive has on their life.

If you sincerely want to become a happy person read and put into practice what you have just learned. Especially practice the exercise described. If you use this exercise while in a deep state of self-hypnosis, the experience will be more realistic and effective. Repeat this program frequently. In a relatively short time you will begin to feel truly happy.

Many of our responses to supposed affronts have been learned over a long period of time. These responses have become habits in us and such habits are actually harmful to ourselves. Anger and hatred produce both mental and physical maladies. Most of these habits were ingrained in our minds by the spoken feelings and physical behavior of our parents and teachers.

Learn to recognize that many of the responses and feelings you have were not invented and rationally analyzed by you. Recall the attitudes, beliefs and behavior of the people who influenced your thinking when you were very young. These attitudes were not always good for you to accept and imitate.

To clarify your thinking in this regard you should again write down the things these people said and did. It is easier to explore these feelings if they are written down so that you can take your time deciding which negative thought patterns had a definite influence on you. Try to recall if these people were happy and successful. Do you really want to be like them? Decide what is best for you and make a determined effort to rid yourself of the traits that you recognize as being negative and harmful.

Racial bigotry is an example of a learned behavior and has caused much suffering for many people. When exposed to clear and rational thinking, those people who possess the feelings of bigotry are able to realize what an unfounded, pointless behavior it is.

Religious bigotry is also a terrible malady that has caused the misery and death of untold numbers of others.

All types of bigotry are learned behaviors that spread hatred and mistrust in the world. These intolerances in our society are unlikely to disappear soon. We can change this pattern of thinking in ourselves, and through good example, possibly influence others to rid themselves of such harmful reasoning.

Your happiness and success in this life depends on ridding your mind of negative, harmful rationalizing by replacing these habits with genuine uplifting beliefs and behavior.

Chapter 12
WAKE UP AND GET REAL!!!
(Eliminating Hypersuggestiblity)

The map is not the territory.
- Alfred Korzbyski.

We alone are responsible for making the choice in our lives to be happy and for being in control of our emotions. Control and choice afford us a wonderful freedom to enjoy our lives. Clear, rational thinking can be achieved if you understand the reasons for confusion and negative thinking. Most of our waking time, we are confronted with negative suggestions from other people and from our own self-doubts. Fear and anxiety cause us to feel helpless and unhappy. These conditions seem too strong to overcome and the main reason for our failure to take control of our feelings is called *hyper-suggestibility.* In this condition we are easily influenced by erroneous concepts from without and within.

People have a tendency to overcomplicate their lives and fail to reduce thoughts to simple reality. We can rid ourselves of these negative feelings and beliefs through the process of deprogramming. Deprogramming will be one of the most important tools to be used for reaching true happiness.

Taking responsibility for making sane, rational decisions will return us to a state of being in which we are truly in control of our lives.

To understand and use deprogramming effectively we need to have a clear picture of what hypnosis really does. Hypnosis, as pictured in the minds of many, probably would be described as a state of trance-like obedience to the will of the hypnotist. Stage shows demonstrating hypnosis are very misleading causing many audience members to leave with strange and negative concepts or misgivings regarding this altered state of consciousness.

In actuality the vast majority of people are always aware of where they are and what is taking place around them while in hypnosis. This leads quite a few to believe that they are not and cannot be hypnotized. The fact is everyone can be hypnotized and most go into that state an average of sixteen times a day. Since we go in and out of hypnosis naturally there remains no reason why we cannot induce it ourselves at any time we choose.

In early mans brain before logic had developed, he had the instincts of an animal, which are referred to as the fight or flight syndrome. When confronted with danger he instinctively reacted by fighting or running away. If he were strong enough he would choose to fight and use violence against an enemy. If he were fleet of foot he would simply run away from the danger.

As time passed the primitive mans' brain slowly developed logic and began to make choices. He discovered how to make use of available weapons against an enemy. He also found safety in numbers and by banding together, primitive men facing the danger together, found that by combining their strength were able to defeat a dangerous animal or even other men who threatened them.

The rational mind also continued to develop but the primitive mind remained, and today still resides in the brain of modern man. Let's take a look at the primitive mind.

Attention needs to be noted on primitive mans' ability to employ the tactic of "playing dead" in response to perceived life threatening experiences, as well as his fight or flight reaction. In this scenario, primitive mans' mind reacted much like some animals react when threatened by a predator. Freezing motionless, remaining that way until the danger or threat has passed. In modern society the fight or flight reaction became less socially acceptable. The rational mind began to devise other means of coping with fear producing circumstances, compromise and negotiation became options unfortunately it also retained the response of mentally playing dead.

At the level of the primitive mind is the autonomic nervous system, comprised of the *sympathetic and parasympathetic nervous systems,* which help control the function of our organs, our involuntary reactions and the fight or flight syndrome.

The socialization of man led to the development of the conscious, thinking and rational part of our brain that we refer to as, the conscious mind.

It perceives emotions, makes judgments and decisions and places a restraint over the subconscious mind's tendency toward the fight or flight reaction. These allusions are a bit overstated here as we only have one brain. Very simply, the sub-conscious and conscious minds are both functions of one whole brain.

In order to differentiate between the various activities of the brain, we refer to the rational thinking behavioral control as the conscious mind and to the primitive instinctive behavioral activities in our brain as the subconscious mind.

The instinctive part of our brain, (subconscious mind) acts like a great and efficient storage bank in a vast computer, holding every experience and thought we have ever been exposed to. It does not posses the power to judge. It merely receives, records and reacts to beliefs that have been programmed and stored. It always cooperates with these beliefs and does all in its power to fulfill them.

The dangers and threats we normally face in our society today are generally fears and worries of a nature that makes them impossible to physically fight against or run away from. With these options denied us we revert to the primitive mind's other alternative, playing dead.

In other words to reach a state of quiet in which our conscious mind is unable to make clear judgments. We enter into a state of *hyper-suggestibility* wherein we allow all sorts of negative input to enter into and be stored in our brain. When our minds are bombarded by the massive amount of information, noise and worries coming from our environment, coupled with our physical discomforts and awareness of our own bodily functions and feelings, our brains overload and escape into the primitive mind. This causes a semi trance like state in which we become easy targets for the reception of negative suggestions.

This same overloading takes place under a controlled environment when working with a hypnotist. The key word is controlled, because in the ensuing *hyper- suggestive* state, we become very relaxed, and the input of suggestions is positive and for our own welfare.

Well-educated and experienced hypnotherapists teach us to be aware of the state of *hyper-suggestibility* and the state of conscious control of our ability to accept or reject suggestions. They point out that our subconscious mind absorbs both positive and negative information alike and that since most people today unknowingly are living their lives in a state of semi-hypnosis, they become extremely vulnerable to suggestion. By strengthening the mind through positive suggestion we can teach it to avoid being so readily affected by the negatives.

The advertising media are well aware of this mental state and they use the knowledge of this condition to their full advantage in order to sell products. They know that people are very open to suggestion. These money-oriented and very astute people use this knowledge to design and implement advertising campaigns for companies that go so far as to make people feel guilty if they fail to use a particular company's products.

The media gurus use anything they can to influence us, like protecting the health of our families and looking out for their safety, or generally improving their standard of living as well as their self esteem and ultimate happiness.

The methods utilized are so insidious and well designed that the public believes that they have made a wise decision to buy. In actuality they have had their emotions manipulated and the decision to buy has not really been judged by their own conscious mind.

Politicians have relied on this weakness throughout history. Instead of calm, clear, rational thinking, a huge number of voters swallow the campaign promises on an emotional level. When the government can so easily manipulate us it leaves almost no wonder that we have so many problems in our lives. It appears that a vast majority of the population wants "Big Brother" to make their decisions for them. It appears so much easier to avoid the responsibility of rational decision-making.

One of the problems involved lies in the fact that people do not realize that they are existing in a state of mild hypnosis most of their lives. This state opens the mind to the reception of suggestions that are not necessarily to their benefit. To really improve our own welfare and the welfare of our nation we must overcome this dilemma and think rationally and be willing to accept the responsibility this requires.

One of the most important duties of the hypnotist is to train the subject to awaken from the trance like state of escape and return fully and completely to the real conscious control of our alert mind. We train ourselves to only return to the hypnotic state when consciously wishing to do so for positive programming exercises.

In the chapter on self-hypnosis, you will recall that the final instructions are to repeat to yourself strongly, "WIDE AWAKE!, WIDE AWAKE!" This returns us to conscious control and eliminates the possibility of accepting any negative suggestions. Another command to yourself is to say "COME UP TO PRESENT, NOW!" This awakens the conscious part of the brain and, with constant practice, will eliminate hyper- suggestibility. This demonstrates important cues used in this method for deprogramming the hypnotic state.

This very effective exercise should be used often during the day. It will result in returning control to the conscious mind.

Instead of getting bogged down in senseless detail we become more able to see the simple truth and make clear, competent, decisions.

We can choose to live a happier, more productive life, by not allowing others to have too great an influence over us.

The muscles in our bodies require exercise to stay in functional and peak condition. The failure to use and tone these muscles causes them to weaken and atrophy. The same activities apply to our minds. The mind should be exercised constantly and this can be accomplished in many ways.

Reading instead of watching television causes us to use our mind to understand the material contained in books, magazines and newspaper articles. As we read we should constantly question the ideas and statements presented and make ourselves judge what we read with a mind to either accept or reject the material. We have the freedom to make our own decisions. Everyone should read some scientific, political or philosophical material each week. Our attempt to understand unfamiliar information is an excellent means of developing our mental muscles.

Keeping a daily journal or just writing down our own opinions of people and situations is also a great way to put our conscious minds to work. Some detailed exercises for this are described in chapter nineteen.

Pursuing a hobby will always keep the mind alert. Any hobby that requires us to learn more information will keep the mind focused and functioning. I experienced this personally when I chose to learn to repair and refinish golf clubs. This hobby forced me to learn unfamiliar techniques as well as technical knowledge needed to accomplish reasonably good results.

This hobby necessitated working with my hands as well as my brain. Hand and eye coordination was improved as a byproduct of this activity. When you are able to reach a good degree of ability to produce acceptable results at your chosen hobby you will experience a deep satisfaction as well as an alert conscious awareness of what you are doing.

Learn to focus on details when you look at anything. This is a mental exercise that supplies valuable training to the conscious mind. It is interesting that different people have such a wide variety of opinions about what they are physically observing. Instead of permitting the objects you look at to enter your mind in a blurry fashion, take the time to focus on the details of what you are seeing. Become very discriminating about what you believe you see. When you really observe details in an unhurried way you will detect things that others miss. You will also develop a greater appreciation for your own sense of sight.

Be sure to remain aware of the present time in an alert fashion. Take control of your conscious awareness and enjoy the freedom and happiness you deserve.

Chapter 13
PREDATORS

Advertising may be described as the science of arresting the human intelligence long enough to get money from it.
- Stephen Leacock

The art of being happy does not depend on the amount of money you have. You do need the necessities of life to avoid feeling unhappy and there are some people in this world that, without remorse or hesitation, will try to take even these away from you. Food, clothing, shelter, education, medical insurance, plus some extra cash for entertainment, give us a secure feeling and more time to spend being happy.

We will have more fun if we pursue an occupation in which we enjoy the work and also take a sense of pride in what we do. The more money we have gives us the freedom to enjoy quality time with those we love.

Most people in society are honest and well meaning, so we are sometimes taken off guard by the few dishonest characters that we encounter. Like sharks in the ocean and tigers in the jungle, these folks are predators.

Their ability to damage us will vary in degree and the people who do this will range from merchandisers to con artists and all the shades of gray in between.

This chapter will help you recognize and avoid the pitfalls that will be used in an effort to take advantage of your own good nature. The ability to see your own weaknesses and develop an awareness of the unscrupulous fellows that try to use you will greatly minimize their ability to rob you of your dignity, as well as your money. The wiser and more discerning you become, the greater chance you have of pulling the fangs out of the predators.

The advertising industry hires masters of manipulation to design and run their campaigns. They are extremely good at getting people to spend scads of money on things they do not really need. Take some time to look at magazine ads and TV commercials. Be very objective and separate the very personal and psychological suggestions from their real bottom line goals, which focus on luring you into buying their product or service. When you remove the hype and get down to the product itself, the compulsion to buy evaporates. You can then make a rational and usually wise decision.

Ask yourself a simple question. Do I really need or want this product? I got by without this product for a long time. I never saw anything like this in my life before. I wonder how I ever got along without it. If I got by without this product or service before, why do I need it now?

Is the product or service worth the price they are asking? Standing back for a while has saved people more "buyer's remorse" than you can imagine. Have you purchased items or services on an emotional impulse in the past and then wished you had walked away from the sale? Most of us, if not all of us, have experienced this situation and from personal and vicarious experience, I can say that it causes great unhappiness. You are better off taking your time to evaluate whether or not a product or service you are considering is truly worth having. Find out if you really want or need the item or service and also throw price into the equation. The cost factor alone may play an important role in your purchasing decision.

Sellers also know that with money back guarantees, less than two percent of the consumers will ever ask for a refund. The longer the guarantee is, the less likely that the seller will ever have to honor it. This "lull them to sleep psychology" works very well and advertisers know this. Everyone has been a victim of slick advertising at one time or another. The key point to be recognized lies not in the fact that we have all been victims, but more so in the idea that the practice of being more aware and prudently selective in the buying choices we make, will protect us from making unwise decisions.

Outside of the corporate sellers you must be very aware of the people you come in contact with face to face. Learn to recognize the people that are trying to take advantage of you and utilize the necessary means to avoid them. Professional con men attempt to take advantage of our weaknesses. These people really understand psychology better than anyone. They explore human weakness and frailty and once exposed to an individual they use their expertise to find their weakest link. They are consummate actors and you will find them to be very likable and personable. They are fun to be around. They specialize in making you feel good and important. They are able to insinuate their way into your life so easily that you will believe they have become your closest friend and ally.

You will not even want to hear anything bad about them from other people. Perhaps you have already met one and maybe still know him or her. These people have specific goals and well-rehearsed plans to achieve them. These are people we all should be wary of when we discover them. The best thing to do with folks like this…. avoid them.

Even after being burned by a con-man most people find themselves too ashamed to admit they had been bilked, even to the point of making excuses for the con-man's behavior. This allows many of these "users" to remain free to ply their trade.

Think of the people in your life that have unfairly used you for one purpose or another. Little children are very adept at manipulating elders in order to get their own way. There is usually someone in your circle of friends that does this much better than most. See people in an objective light and their flaws will become clearer.

There have been many reported cases of men and women losing their life savings to unscrupulous people who got them to invest in one scheme or another.

These shadowy investments, which promised high returns in short periods of time, are definitely illegal. The operators of these scams are usually long gone before their victims realize they had been swindled.

One of the favorite targets of swindlers is lonely women, especially those with money and property. They prey upon the emotions of these unfortunate ladies, ingratiating themselves to a point where the women begin to have absolute trust in them.

The con-man may suggest marriage or a business venture or any other concept that his victim accepts as a good reason to contribute money or other assets for. The swindler may even insinuate that the money is to be used for religious purposes or a charitable cause. These people use romance and flattery to get their way. Often they play on the victim's own greed, promising fantastic returns on investments. When the people thus manipulated begin to realize that they have been duped, the money and the swindler have both disappeared. Law enforcement agencies throughout the country are kept very busy trying to warn people of these dangers but also trying to apprehend the criminal. In most cases the money will never be recovered even if the perpetrator has been put in jail.

Generally if people are aware of their own weaknesses they will avoid allowing themselves to be defrauded. You needn't be paranoid about this unconscionable activity of swindlers. Become aware of your own weakness and susceptibility and refuse to let others take advantage of them.

How can I protect myself from a predator?

Certain traits can be readily observed, so watch for the following:

- **If it sounds too good to be true, it is probably a lie.**
- **How did this person insinuate himself or herself into my life?**
- **Honestly, am I really so great that I attracted this person to me?**
- **Am I as wonderful to be around as this person leads me to believe?**
- **What are they after? (They will be giving you clues to this very subtly and very often).**

To defend yourself you must honestly analyze your own traits and weaknesses, be objective, write them down. Find out your own weakest points and then we can change that vulnerability. The only way to protect yourself from predators lies in the formulation of a game plan. This plan will be focused on strengthening resistance to your vulnerabilities in conjunction with improving your ability to view others more objectively.

Suggestions

- **Do I want something for nothing? (Who doesn't?).**
- **Am I a lonely person and feel a void that needs to be filled?**
- **Do I have assets that others might want to tap into?**
- **Do I reveal myself by talking too much about myself? (Free information for the con man).**
- **Am I a compulsive gambler?**
- **Do I need someone to protect me?**
- **Am I a bleeding heart for a sad story?**

There are other weaknesses and you will recognize them when you are honest with yourself. Write them down. Using our visualization tool, we set out to change these human weaknesses in ourselves with really powerful, wise qualities, until we truly believe these changes completely. One by one these weak traits will go away. Use self-hypnosis and visualization and reinforcement as the main tools. These, in combination with the previous game plan mentioned, need to be directed toward finding and eradicating weaknesses, while at the same time allowing the exercise of a more objective view when dealing with others. Reprogram your mind by the use of self-hypnosis (chapter 3) and common sense (chapter 4). The predator is lazy by nature, and once or twice turned down will go after easier prey. His true nature will be seen. He doesn't have to hide it anymore because he gave up the effort of trying to con or manipulate your newer, wiser self.

Chapter 14
FALSE CRUTCHES
(Drug and alcohol dependence)

You may have to fight a battle more than once to win it.
- Margaret Thatcher.

The people who have developed an addiction to drugs and alcohol have limited their options in life to only one thing, the chemical they have grown to depend on for escape from their problems. These people feel unable to function or feel comfortable without the use of these false crutches. These poisonous substances are being used to temporarily overcome a feeling of emotional, physical or mental pain. They hold a false, insidious belief in their own minds that they need the drug(s) they are taking. The addiction comes down to limiting themselves to only one option, the use of the chemical involved. People in this situation require the drugs they take just to function.

Actually there are many options to overcoming the feelings of inadequacy, fear, loneliness and pain. People who suffer from severe physical pain are apt to become dependent on prescription drugs to alleviate that condition. When dependence has been created and the source of over-the-counter medicine has been cut off, this can often lead many people to experiment with the use of illegal substances while in search of similar effects to the prescribed drugs.

To make the situation worse, the ingestion of these drugs accompanied by alcohol has been shown to be dangerously life threatening. Through thousands of autopsies we are finding that drinking alcohol with illegal drugs is not uncommon.

K.C., of KC and the Sunshine Band, was an example of what can happen when people come under a great deal of stress and choose the wrong means of handling it. In his television interview he told of the breakup of the band and how he tried to succeed apart from them. Apparently this didn't work out very well for K.C. After a lackluster attempt of going on his own he was severely injured in a head on auto collision that left him partially paralyzed and in great pain. This required a lot of courage on his part to go through the rehabilitation period that lasted around nine months.

During that time he was on prescription pain medication. After this, the death of his father affected him very deeply and an attempt at his comeback in the music world was accompanied by pain medication, and as he put it, "A hundred thousand dollar a year habit of non-prescription drugs." Added to this, he said, was around a fifth a day alcohol habit. On occasion, he said, he had black out periods and grand mal seizures from which he nearly died. This frightened him greatly. With the help of his family and friends and his own determination he overcame the addictions.

He realized that music and his being able to perform, was more important to him than an escape through the use of adverse chemicals. During his recovery a friend pointed out that some of the newer bands were imitating the music that the Sunshine Band had pioneered. This was a boost in that he was able to give people the real thing instead of an imitation.

K.C. had options throughout this time but an addict fails to see but one course, the short-term escape from his problems through chemical dependency. K.C. should be greatly commended for the very open sharing of his story with the public and for his will and courage to fight and overcome his addictions.

Alcohol and drugs are sometimes used as a replacement for courage or an escape from pain, emotional or physical. Addiction adds another emotional stress, as fearing the time when the effects of the drug wear off. Addiction also has an extremely adverse effect on the physical body and can certainly lead to death.

Using alcohol or drugs to overcome insecurity at work or in social situations leads into a habit and the habit leads into addiction. If the addict tries to quit, reverse reactions occur. His original feelings of unhappiness and insecurity seem to be much stronger than before and he returns to his addiction. When the addict is forced to go without his drug he loses his false sense of security. This places him face to face with his original pain and unhappiness.

When he finally seeks help he needs to be taught to see that he is a worthwhile person with many fine qualities that need to be strengthened and bolstered. His perception of himself must be nurtured into seeing himself as a person he likes and respects.

Overcoming addiction should not be considered a job for self-help alone. The person in this condition needs professional help and a great deal of love and encouragement from family and friends. We all need a shoulder to cry on, a person to listen to us and someone who can relate to the problem we are facing.

Many fine programs are available to help with the addicts' recovery. New drugs and procedures along with the growing awareness by the medical profession of this problem should be an encouragement to the addict who wants to recover. Good hypnotherapists can help in locating the underlying causes of the addiction. They can also assist in the emotional and psychological improvement through the use of suggestions given under hypnosis to bolster the patients self esteem and will to recover.

Even psychiatrists use hypnosis to aid in treatment as well as administering short-term use of prescription drugs. They use hypnosis as a short cut or more immediate pathway into the mind with hopes of locating the cause of the addiction.

Spiritual counseling by well-trained ministers is also of great value for restoring the addicts self esteem and purpose in his life. Seeking the help of others we believe in can offer hope, and much needed guidance. The addict may require more than most.

One of the greatest organizations which has shown tremendous success in people's recovery is Alcoholics Anonymous. The twelve steps in their program along with their mutual support and ability to relate directly to the problem, has done wonders for hundreds of thousands of people. For alcoholics that really want to quit drinking I suggest investigating what they have to offer. Most religious leaders and most doctors refer recovering alcoholics to A.A. as a program that really does work.

Under the guidance of a qualified hypnotherapist the patient may use self-hypnosis to strengthen his resolve to be drug and alcohol free and to improve his own self-esteem. Once a person learns self-hypnosis, they can call on the use of it at any time, to help them reinforce their goal of staying sober.

People do have options to solve their problems and these should be located and used before a person develops a habit that might lead to addiction. No matter what the financial cost or time that may be involved, your life is worth finding a way to solve your problems without the use of drugs.

Through years of observation and study I have concluded that sudden life changes relating to notoriety coupled with pressures of the need to be constantly creative in ones occupation, promote the apparent need and means for drug and alcohol addiction. This seems to be prevalent in the entertainment industry.

When a person makes the giant leap from obscurity and poverty to wealth and fame he is placed in a very unfamiliar life style. Demands on his time by fans, producers, agents, movie studios and record companies, are bound to cause confusion, fatigue and a general sense of identity loss in nearly all but the most solidly adjusted people. Anyone in the position of possibly becoming a celebrity should be aware of the life changes he will be facing. Being prepared for these alterations in existence will require an extraordinary commitment to self-discipline and personality transformation.

Children growing up without a true sense of moral and ethical values are faced with the temptation to experiment with illegal and harmful substances.

Poverty and the feelings of helplessness and hopelessness induce many to seek an escape through the use of drugs and alcohol. Drug dealers make it cheap and easy for these young people to obtain drugs. When they become addicts they have become slaves to the drugs and the drug dealers. They are led into a life of criminal activities and prostitution in order to pay for their addiction.

Peer group pressure has an influence on these children as well. This becomes a hell on earth for far too many kids. Drug awareness programs are doing a wonderful job but the fantastic financial rewards for the drug lords and the dealers continue to keep them in business.

Obviously, to educate young people into the realization that a better, happier way to live actually does exist without having to be under the influence of drugs and alcohol and will prove the wisest course for the future. These awareness programs are supported and often conducted by church groups, hospitals and law enforcement agencies.

Addiction is a very difficult subject to face, but everyone in our society must address it. We are all in trouble not only from the threat of our own possible addiction, but because we are in grave danger from criminal actions by people seeking money through illegal means in order to obtain their drugs. The suggestions in this chapter have already outlined the tools I feel are necessary to cope with addiction.   It can be overcome. Successful recovery from addiction demonstrates a truly tremendous accomplishment and will greatly improve ones chances of leading a happy and productive life.

Chapter 15
SPORTS PSYCHOLOGY

Do you know what my favorite part of the game is? The Opportunity to play.

- Mike Singletary

Sports Psychology is both a science and an art. It is a mental discipline that causes a vast improvement in physical performance. The sports psychologist trains the athlete to allow his subconscious mind to control the actions of his muscles while keeping the conscious mind from interfering. This training results in the athlete being able to achieve his optimum performance the majority of the time. When the subconscious mind is in control of the physical activity the responses related to the sport appear to be both fluid and effortless. Most athletes have experienced this occurrence many times.

In the sports of boxing, judo and other types of hand to hand combat, the athlete has trained his subconscious mind through constant repetition of the necessary movements to a point where action and reaction become instinctive. Trying to control these movements consciously only tenses the muscles and interferes with the smooth, powerful and lightning fast actions desired.

In order for us to better understand the application of sports psychology let's take a look at the needs and aspirations of a professional athlete to see how these techniques help him become more proficient and successful. Since many professional athletes have openly discussed the fact that they employ a sports psychologist, the amateur athlete has been wondering if he should do this. Psychology has actually contributed much to athletic performance.

In the old days, pep talks, rallies and adrenaline producing gyrations were thought to be the answer. These are still powerful motivators and have a definite place in all sports fields. The sports psychologist utilizes different tools and methods to derive desired results.

The tremendous pressure that professional athletes perform under is beyond the imagination of the ordinary person. Besides having great pride in what they do the professional athlete also needs to stay at his peak for monetary reasons. How long will his body carry him along? The professional athlete needs to excel in as short a time as possible. For some players, this leads to endorsements from various manufacturers, cereal companies, makers of sports equipment, country clubs and others trying to capitalize on the athlete's notoriety. But, the professional athlete must disconnect himself from pressures or other distracting thoughts that might hamper his ability to let the inner computer, or subconscious mind, do all the work without interference from the conscious mind.

Whether a professional or an amateur, certain tools are required for the individual to attain success. Better equipment, better health, better training and more knowledge are some of these tools. There is also a definite need for better mental discipline. It is always important to clearly visualize a picture of what you wish to accomplish. For some people this is very easy to do. If you have difficulty seeing a picture in your mind, I suggest the following exercises. Everyone is able to develop the ability to visualize.

Close your eyes and see the face of a clock in your mind in detail. Look at the position of the hour and minute hands and watch the second hand as it travels around the dial. Repeat this several times.

Picture in your mind a box with the lid off. Visualize placing a gift for a friend into the box. See yourself putting the lid on the box. Now see a roll of gift wrapping paper and look at its pattern and color. Visualize yourself wrapping the box with the paper and then place a bow and card on the newly wrapped gift. Repeat this several times until these pictures become easy to produce in your mind.

In sports before performing, close your eyes and see a clear picture of what you wish to accomplish, several times.

This is a mental rehearsal of what you plan to do. Now open your eyes and allow your inner mind make it happen, just the way you mentally rehearsed it.

A friend of mine was playing a practice round of golf with Jack Nicklaus. Jack always stood over a putt far longer than anyone else on the tour. My friend asked him what he was thinking when he stood there so long. Nicklaus told him that he was visualizing the putt in his mind, the ball following a specific line and falling into the cup. He said that when he finally stroked the putt his chances of success were much greater as he had already made the putt four times in his mind.

To get a clearer idea of how these factors are applied let's use the sport of golf as an example.

Caddies play an important part in the sport of golf. Prior to each round played the caddy walks the course, jots down landmarks, pin positions on each green and the distances to these pins from every angle. He notes hidden dangers, consistency of sand traps, conditions of fairways, greens and so on.

A good, knowledgeable caddie is always in demand. Caddies for the highly successful players are paid a percentage of the winnings and if they are that good, their professional takes them to every event he plays in. In effect, they perform as a team.

On the course the pro asks the caddie the distance to the pin from where the ball lies. The professional has his own information and they compare notes. They are usually within a few yards of each other's calculations. The golf pro knows how far he hits a specific club under various conditions, so this provides valuable information to improve his performance.

<u>Why should a professional need a sports psychologist?</u>

The professional, just another human being, lacks the qualities which enable machines to work from the necessary data alone with no interference from anything else affecting its performance. The athlete faces a tremendous amount of pressure. Under pressure to perform, all of us will tend to force the issue. The conscious mind actually puts tension into the muscles being used in this situation thereby interfering with the optimum performance necessary to achieve success.

Have you ever heard an athlete say he was playing in the zone? The sports psychologist's job requires him to act as a trainer to put the athlete in the zone and keep him playing in that zone.

What do we mean when we refer to the "zone?"

The athlete usually doesn't know what the zone is, or how he got there. He perceives it as a feeling in his body and mind. The zone constitutes a condition in which the conscious ego divorces itself from the subconscious control of the muscles being used. The conscious mind merely feeds in information without making any interfering judgments. It resembles data entry on a computer.

The subconscious mind then commands the muscles without any indecision and at a speed at least 10 times faster than the conscious mind could possibly achieve. The subconscious mind, or inner computer, merely drives the program and doubt fails to penetrate it. The subconscious mind stands alone as the one part of our brain that performs most nearly like a machine. It remains unaware that it performs under pressure. It merely collates and organizes the data, and then pushes all the right buttons at the right time. This gives the muscles the freedom to react in such a way as to produce the more desirable result.

Do I need a sports psychologist in order to improve my performance? Possibly, but they cost money. You can still accomplish a lot on your own.

Clearly understand the concept of allowing the subconscious mind to take control. Then go to Chapter 3 and use the self-hypnosis and visualization methods until you truly master them. Apply the proper visualization to your own game and repeat that exercise often. You will then begin to experience your sport from a new and exciting perspective.

The athlete must be well versed in the basics of the sport he plays. He must train himself to perform as well as possible. He should also be in the best physical condition he can attain. Training in any sport can be considered very similar to learning to drive a car. When you first started your muscles were tense because your conscious mind was in control and you thought about all the things you had to perform. You probably over-compensated the use of the steering wheel, clutch, accelerator and brakes.

All during this time the subconscious mind was absorbing the lessons you were learning. Like many other activities we learn, the inner computer in your brain began to take over the task of performing the functions needed to drive the car. It became so good at this that in time you could be thinking about something entirely different and your subconscious mind drove the car better than you could by consciously trying to control it.

If you tried to consciously control the utensils you use when eating, you would more than likely stab yourself in the cheek with your fork.

When your inner computer has learned a sport and your conscious mind allows the subconscious mind to function without interference, you will continue to improve at your game. Use the self-hypnosis technique you learned in chapter 3. Reach a comfortable working state for visualization and begin picturing in your mind as realistically as possible the performance of your game. Employing the senses of sight, sound, smell, taste and feel will make this most effective. You can actually practice your activity in your mind and this will affect the muscles as they respond almost imperceptibly during the session. You might consider it muscle training.

When you go out to physically engage in the sport, learn by practice to keep your conscious mind from interfering with your subconscious mind's control. Distracting the mind by giving it a task not directly related to your action can help you accomplish this.

As an example: in golf, when getting ready to make a putt, first feed in information to the subconscious by looking at the line to the hole from different angles but don't judge. Walk the distance to the hole and allow information to be fed in by the feeling through your feet. Again don't judge or let your ego interfere. Ego interference will taint the effects of your subconscious mind's recent gathering of information.

When you are ready to putt the ball, pay attention to the prompting of the subconscious to possibly shift your feet, realign the putter face etc. Distract the conscious mind from interfering with the stroke by giving it a task. The task requires you to mentally go over to the cup, bend down and pick the ball up out of the hole. During this time you have allowed the inner computer to control the muscles and make the stroke. The results will be far better than you have been used to. With practice you will see a gradual but noticeable improvement in your game. An important thing to remember will be forcing yourself to divorce your ego from your performance. This opens the doorway to enter into and play in the "zone."

The implementation of sports psychology gives an added advantage to a team as well as to an individual player.

Application To Team Sports *(Football)*

Practice self-hypnosis until you develop the ability to reach a mild hypnotic state. Hypnosis opens a channel to your subconscious mind. This state makes the programming (learning) take place rapidly and effectively. In this altered and focused condition your inner computer absorbs and records the visual images you wish to program.

You must be in a mild hypnotic state for this programming to be effective. Now you will be able to program the subconscious mind. Watch a sport instructional videotape that has an athlete involved that you would like to emulate. By observing this tape, your subconscious mind will, through exposure to this vicarious data, begin to assimilate that athlete's style and eventually be able to emulate his performance as well.

The subconscious mind does not have the ability to tell the difference between a vividly imagined event and reality. Knowledge of this fact makes it easy to improve at any sport by continual programming of your inner computer.

Choosing a Role Model

Choose an athlete that you would most like to copy in performance. When deciding on a role model, look for an athlete that has a temperament close to your own, preferably someone with a similar physical build and also one that plays the same position in team sports as yourself.

By diligent searching you will be able to locate videotapes of your role model and these should be the ones you use. You can videotape a game in which your role model is playing right onto your VCR.

If you are a defensive back or defensive end or tackle or linebacker, obtain a tape of the athlete you want to become most like. Watch these tapes in a mild state of hypnosis. Do not try to analyze their movements consciously. Imagine that you are already the athlete you are watching.

Your subconscious mind will absorb the movements, physical moods and characteristics of your role model whether in action or in his demeanor between plays. Vividly imagine the gestures, facial expressions, body language and even perceived emotions of that athlete. Feel what you are watching just as if this is happening physically to your own body. Feel that you are actually the athlete in the videotape. During your observation of the plays in progress, there will be almost imperceptible movements in your own muscles, mimicking what you're seeing, and these feelings will be transmitted and stored in your subconscious computer.

You must practice this procedure repeatedly. Do not analyze what the role model is doing. Feel what he is doing. Conscious analysis directly interferes with this method of programming.

You will soon find yourself, when in the actual game or during a scrimmage, performing in ways very similar to the role model you have chosen without consciously thinking of the moves you are making. When the subconscious mind is in control of the action the mental commands to the muscles become ten times more rapid than if you had to think about it. The more you are able to identify with your role model, the better player you will become.

Whether you are an offensive, defensive or special team's player, this method of training works exactly the same way. You will get the urge to put in extra practice time, spend more time in the weight room, do more wind sprints and study your playbook. It doesn't hurt to know what every player on the team is supposed to be doing. All the great players are aware of what their teammates are doing on every designed play.

A good athlete always works very hard on the basics of his sport. Basics are the foundations of good performance. This training develops sound basics, excellent physical conditioning, mental toughness and exceptional self-confidence. You will excel rapidly as an athlete by repeatedly programming your inner computer.

Discuss this training with your coaches. They are able to see things from the outside and will help you with your performance. Be sure of this. Your coach wants you to become as good as you can possibly be at your sport.

All great coaches use every means they can find to improve team performance.

If a player is a prima donna with an attitude that is disruptive to the team, he will overcome that problem by changing the attitude of the player or by getting rid of him. A team sport requires the best efforts of all its players working together for the good of the entire team.

The players that are most committed to the success not only of themselves but also of their teammates prove to be the most valuable assets the coach can have.

There is no star running back in the NFL that could be a star without the great blocking of his offensive line and the blocking of other running backs, tight ends and wide receivers. Coaches know that without great linemen doing their jobs right, they would never win a game.

Coaching

A head coach is responsible for the success of his team. In professional sports the head coach has many assistants such as special team coaches, offensive and defensive coaches, line coaches, trainers and so on. The final responsibility of the performance of the team is directly on the shoulders of the head coach. When choosing his assistants he must obtain people that support his own program. He needs to be able to trust in and communicate with his assistants. He must be able to delegate responsibility with the assurance that his coaches will do their job capably and wisely. The head coach must also keep an open mind in order to accept ideas and suggestions the assistants have to offer him. The final decisions however are his to make.

Team Sports Psychology requires that all the coaches be involved in applying this concept, not only to the players but to themselves as well. Anything that has ever been achieved first had to be conceived and believed in the mind. Goals must be set and plans made for reaching these goals. The desired result must be believed and there must be a total commitment to carrying out the plan. Visualizing the desired goal is just as effective and necessary for the coaching staff as it is for the players. This program, put into practice, develops a tremendous sense of self-confidence and team confidence. This positive belief will be transmitted from the coaching staff to the team. Attitudes will be both calm and positive.

Every coach and every player will have a clear understanding of their goals and responsibilities. This is an interactive program and it will dynamically improve the character and performance of the team.

What does this chapter have to do with becoming successful and happy? If you enjoy playing any sport, and suddenly, with very little effort on your part, you begin to excel, don't you think a happy smile is going to show up on your face? It is a rewarding experience to become as good as you can be.

Chapter 16
LETS BE PALS

A friend is one who knows us, but loves us anyway.
Fr. Jerome Cummings.

Many fine books have been written about this subject such as, "How to Win Friends and Influence People." Most of these volumes are very long and tedious to read.

In this chapter I have outlined the simplest way to acquire and keep new friends. One quality that we all seek to have is a happy, positive, outgoing personality. We are attracted to a person that exudes these traits.

In order to attract new friends, we must first become a true friend to ourselves. Unless we can accomplish this first task any means we employ to attract others will be seen as false and manipulative. To become a true friend to oneself will prove the most difficult task to be faced.

We must be aware of our shortcomings and become honestly committed to changing these flaws into positive traits. We all have many good qualities, which, through false humility, we tend to play down. If you find difficulty in accepting a sincere and personal compliment, you have located an area that needs a lot of work.

The best way to begin liking yourself starts with a simple but important exercise. Make out a complete and honest list of your good and bad traits. No one except you should ever see this list. Keep it private and refer to it often. After you have compiled your list, leave room by each trait to make little comments about each trait whether good or bad.

EXAMPLES

BAD TRAIT

I am very critical of others and often hurt their feelings with my words or actions.

COMMENTS

I remember my father being this way with me when I was young. In fact I discovered that I have been using the same words and tone of voice he used. I recognize that this is an acquired habit so before I make any critical statement I will pause and think about what I intend to say. If it will be an offense to someone I remain quiet. I refuse to be a phonograph record replaying my father's behavior.

GOOD TRAIT

I really like people and enjoy their company.

COMMENTS

The best way to please others with comments lies in complimenting their action, not their person. This conveys a very powerful, positive message, without embarrassing the person receiving the compliment. I will speak only honest positive things about others to people they come in contact with. Whatever I say will come back to them, good or bad. Therefore I will make it good.

BAD TRAIT

I talk about myself too much. I can see the glazed look of boredom come over the eyes of the person I am speaking to. They are tired of hearing me and I can't seem to stop talking about ME.

COMMENT

I was given two ears and one mouth for a very good reason, so I would listen twice as much as I talk. Let's put this lesson into practice. In making these lists of good and bad traits my comments about improvement are just common sense.

Think of the things you would like someone else to change about themselves in order to make them more enjoyable to be around. Now that you have analyzed those changes apply them to yourself. This plan functions as a work of true awareness that you will discover to be well worth the effort you put into it.

GET HAPPY

Try to keep a smile on your face as long and as often as you can. Smiles attract other people. Often they will even ask you why you are smiling. Tell them it is because you are happy. When you smile it works inwardly on your psyche and will actually begin to give you a feeling of happiness and confidence.

Look in your mirror often with a great big smile on your face and say, "I really like you." As silly as this may seem it works like magic. It encourages you to like yourself more and it reinforces all the many good traits you already possess. Laugh at yourself if you feel like it. That will also get rid of a lot of negative feelings you might be carrying around. Things will seem a lot less serious to you and this exercise will reduce the feeling of stress by putting problems into a more realistic perspective.

You will discover that many of the things you considered serious problems are not nearly as serious as you had perceived them. Do not fail to practice this exercise no matter how foolish it may seem.

Inside a week you will be achieving a truly happy state of mind. When you use self-hypnosis to build up your good qualities through visualization in your mind to a point of true belief, the less desirable traits will weaken and lose their influence on you.

Apply this to the picture of the personality you wish to possess. Visualize yourself as a happy, self confident, outgoing person. Imagine you are meeting yourself for the first time. See only the good qualities you want to have.

Go into detail in your mind observing all these positive traits as already existing. They probably are even if you have been hiding them from the rest of the world.

See yourself as a person you would really enjoy being with. Have a conversation with yourself and find all the great and good discoveries about you that have been lying dormant. Resolve to bring out all your good qualities for others to see. Picture yourself exactly as you would like to be.

One of the most important tools to use in this book is self-hypnosis. Practice the instructions in chapter three until you have mastered the ability to reach a deep working state of suggestibility.

The result of this visualization process is to program your subconscious mind, to bring about all these wonderful changes. That inner mental computer will perform miracles of transformation in your life. This will occur when you truly believe the changes you wish to make have already been accomplished. Your Invisible Genie (subconscious mind) is just waiting to fulfill your wishes.

LET'S MAKE A FRIEND EXECISE

Try this exercise out on a total stranger.

With a smile on your face, start a conversation with a total stranger about the weather or the place where the two of you are speaking. When they answer you give them your total and undivided attention, with your eyes, ears and a big smile. Encourage the person to talk about themselves about where they came from or what their job is. Ask an impersonal question even if you decide to ask directions and stay attentive to what they say. Try to induce them to talk about anything. This is a challenge for you but it is also a lot of fun to cause them to respond. Avoid interrupting them. All that may be needed is a nod of understanding or possibly a question to prompt them to talk about themselves. Even if they bore you remember this is a training exercise for you and continue to devote your full attention to them and to what they say occasionally making comments to make them fully aware that you are paying attention. Repeat a statement they make. This shows that you are sincerely trying to understand what they are telling you.

Be gracious when you part from them and sincerely thank them for talking with you. You may never see them again but I promise you several things will happen.

As pointed out previously people love to talk about themselves so this experience will have provided a foundation for honing the skills of becoming a good listener. You will always learn something new from people you listen to. You also may have started up a long and lasting friendship.

Make a habit of always being clean, neat, and presentable. Use deodorant and mouthwash. Do not give any physical offense to the eyes, nose, and ears of others.

Stay well informed on current events as these topics come up in many conversations. If you are not well informed on the topic the other person happens to be talking about admit your ignorance and ask them to clarify or in other words teach you. People love to display their knowledge and are delighted to find an eager, willing pupil.

Avoid ever saying bad things about anyone. If you relate good, positive things about others your listener will pick up a good and trusting feeling about you. They will never be worried about your saying derogatory things about them to others; in fact, they will probably expect that you will be saying complimentary things about them. You will have gained their confidence and respect and possibly their friendship.

Always make time for other people. Just think of the time during the day that you waste, when it could have been used to make people feel happier about themselves. When you are able to make others happy you are actually making yourself happy as well.

Don't tell your troubles to anyone except a counselor or a very understanding and patient old friend. People do not want to hear about your problems. They have enough of their own. Tell people you are feeling fine and everything is going great. Constant habitual use of these statements will also convince you that you do feel good and you begin to realize that in all actuality everything is going fine and will continue to improve.

When someone asks you for help, give it freely and do it right away. Other things can be postponed and you can take care of these when you have finished helping your friend. Although the thought of self-benefit should not enter into this picture, it probably will in some form or another. These things are rarely forgotten or dismissed. They are remembered whether or not they are ever mentioned again.

Do not give lip service by saying things you don't really mean. Don't promise help unless you fully intend to give it.

You have surely met someone like this in your life and have experienced disappointment and frustration resulting from phony promises. The words sounded good to you but in fact they would have been better left unsaid. We are all very much alike in our human nature. What we like about another personality usually tends to be what they will like in our own. What we appreciate in their good actions, much like a reflection, are the things they will want to recognize in ours. Make a habit of associating with the happy, positive people and their good qualities will be absorbed by you.

Sometimes we stay around people whose qualities are actually detrimental to our own welfare. Their negative outlook on life and people will be a bad influence on our own attitude. For our own good we must escape the poor influence they have in our lives.

When I was a teaching Golf Professional at Sunset Hills Country Club, I frequently came in contact with many celebrities. I met many of the players from the L.A. Rams and the Dallas Cowboys football teams. It was great fun to listen to them describe what it was like to play in the N.F.L.

These were fantastic guys, just like us but with muscles and talent and with really good contracts too. They were being paid to play the game they loved. We also had a number of movie stars that played our course.

One evening the club manager and I were closing out the cash register for the day when in from their round of golf came Dina Merrill and her husband Cliff Robertson. It was a chilly evening and the coffee shop was already closed. Ed Hogan the manager suggested that I climb over the counter and get the coffeepot and some cups for them. Being young and agile I quickly scrambled over the barrier and came back with the coffee.

Cliff Robertson and his wife insisted I join them at a table. I had seen them both in movies. I really wanted to know more about them but was caught up in Mr. Robertson's dynamic personality.

Before I knew what was happening he had turned the conversation completely around. He asked me all about the course and the membership and most significantly he wanted to know all about me and my wife and our children. He was actually interviewing me and making me feel like a celebrity.

I wasn't given the opportunity to ask questions, I was too busy giving him answers. I felt wonderful and important and had discovered the magic in his personality was his genuine interest in people. Cliff Robertson and Dina Merrill actually enjoyed learning about other people.

I decided that if it was good enough for a famous star to spend his valuable time this way then it was exactly the way I should act toward others. My whole attitude changed as a result of the time I shared coffee with Mr. and Mrs. Robertson. Instead of being the self-important teaching pro I started finding out all I could about my students and all the country club members. I listened to them and made them feel truly important.

I became interested in the people that were my pupils. They deserved to be treated that way. They were not only very important but also very interesting. Soon I was the busiest teaching pro in Ventura County. My students told their friends about me and I was inundated with more pupils than I could imagine. The new people were treated in exactly the same way.

We are all so much alike in our human nature that these lessons apply to us all. We must learn to treat everyone in the same way we want to be treated. We should always be on guard against being wrapped up in ourselves.

I made this mistake when my father passed away. I felt all alone and became withdrawn and depressed. This obviously showed in the way I moped around the course and the Pro Shop. I had many friends that played our course frequently. To my great fortune one of these friends was Dub Taylor, the famous character actor with the thickest southern accent I had ever heard. Dub was never one to hold back his comments when he felt they could help someone. He is the man that gave me the wake up call.

I will never forget Dub calling me aside wind saying, "Son, yo' daddy don' wan' you goin' 'round all sad and depressed. Get that smile back on yo' face and take care of all these people that look up to you." I put that smile back on my face and in my heart. As Dub said, "Yo" daddy is watchin' you." I really believed him.

When you really care about others and focus on helping them you forget all about your own sadness. It is a privilege to be able to help other people.

<u>*Visualization Practice*</u>

The daily practice of these exercises will soon affect you in a profound and positive way.

While in a mild state of hypnosis, imagine yourself in conversations with other people. See yourself as being absorbed in what they are saying, actually enjoying the stories they are telling you.

Feel a joy in just being around others and relating to them. Have a smile on your face as you focus your attention on them. Imagine the things you are saying. You speak in a positive and comfortable manner. See them responding with interest to what you are saying. Through your own body language project an air of friendship. Make this visualization as real as you possibly can, using all of your senses.

Practice this program daily and watch just how happy and successful your life will become. You will be surprised in a short time by the number of people that will seek out your friendship.

Don't stop at the visualization exercise. Put it into action.

Chapter 17
LET'S GET RICH

Money is better than poverty, if only for financial reasons.
- Woody Allen.

There exists a vast reservoir of money in this country and anyone who wants can tap into it. Opportunities abound now more than they ever have in the past. The person that wishes to improve his financial status must do some clear thinking and make some definite decisions. Once these decisions have been made and a plan devised, comes the most important step of all, action. Without persistent and determined action, nothing is going to happen. Devise the plan and then work the plan as if your life depended on it.

Wealth, of itself, will not bring happiness, but it can definitely relieve us from financial distress and worry. Most people just live from payday to payday and watch their budgets closely in order to be able to keep up with the expenses of daily living. In our own minds we have already determined what we are worth financially and our incomes are pretty consistent with the beliefs that we hold. If we wish that we had more money we must realize that a price must be paid to acquire it.

Many of us think that becoming rich relies on luck. This idea couldn't be much further from the real truth. The majority of wealthy people have worked very diligently, following a specific plan to gain their wealth. Many of them took risks that most others would be afraid to try. They were willing to work long hours gaining all the knowledge needed to succeed at the program they chose to follow.

An immediate way to obtain more money presents itself in the form of a second job and accompanying the job with a decision to save this additional income rather than spend it. The added income can then become a source of capital for investing in a project to earn more money. However, if you come across an opportunity to invest and the investment offers a fairly quick return, you might consider borrowing money to invest. Importance must be placed on an awareness of the risks involved before making such a decision.

Most of the wealthy people I know have a great respect for money. They also have a strong tendency to be very frugal. One of the prime strategies they use relies on putting their money to work for them by constantly investing their profits and then reinvesting the profits from those newer investments. In this way they are compounding their income. Unlike most of us, wealthy people are willing to take calculated risks rather than just try to hold onto their earnings, so they constantly put those earnings to work for them. They are also always looking for opportunities to use other people's money for investment as long as they share in the earnings of those investments.

Another very important point to note pertains to the fact that they only involve themselves in ventures with which they are thoroughly familiar rather than gamble on something that shows the promise of a good return, but in which they are not experienced.

The ones who attain wealth are totally focused on a very clear and specific objective and they stay in control of the management of the venture. Attractive, quick-return investments often do not have real substance. No substitute can replace the need for accurate knowledge and hard work. If you feel that you really want to improve your financial status, be prepared to work diligently at understanding all the methods and risks involved in any venture.

Your mind can be programmed to attain great wealth and it will prompt you to do all the things that are necessary to reach the goal you set for yourself. Total belief in the desired outcome will give you the plan and the persistence required to accomplish that goal.

Do not be afraid to take calculated risks. You may fail but you will keep persisting. Keep trying over and over and over. One good success will far more than outweigh any previous losses. Belief in success is the main trait of successful people. They believe and focus their whole attention on the result they desire and keep persisting despite setbacks. Persistence, in spite of resistance, demonstrates their second greatest trait.

I suggest that you use self-hypnosis to set and program a specific goal. Make this goal as real and believable in your programming sessions as is possible. Repetition of the visualization of the ultimate goal desired, as if it has already been accomplished, will put your subconscious mind in high gear. The goal must be specific and the proposed method for reaching that goal should be well defined. It also helps to set a time limit for reaching that goal.

Use as a proposed plan some type of business or service that you are already familiar with. As an example, choose a business that you have been involved in for a long period of time. Talk to others familiar with that type of business to gain further insights. Read everything you can put your hands on relating to that business. Find out all you can about the customers' point of view regarding the business.

What begins to take place is an input of relative facts regarding the business or topic you are researching into the subconscious mind, which will store and collate and eventually employ this information to devise the most effective plan for the achievement of the result you wish to attain.

Using a deep working state of hypnosis, visualize yourself as completely successful. See yourself receiving cash and checks. Make this visualization as real as possible.

Visualize yourself making large bank deposits. Feel the money and checks in your hands. See the large deposits entered in your bankbook. See and feel the new car and house you will own, just as if they were already yours.

See yourself mixing with wealthy influential, friends. See, feel and smell your new clothes. Feel large amounts of money in your pockets. Feel the financial security in your whole being.

Develop in your mind a healthy respect for money and all the changes it will make in your life. Take on a truly believing attitude that you are already financially secure. See money being attracted to you. It comes to you in greater and greater quantities. See yourself making wise, sound and calculated investments. You envision yourself as money orientated, money-wise and financially secure.

Spend at least 15 minutes twice daily in this programming session. Remember that the subconscious mind cannot differentiate between a real event and one that is vividly imagined. It will accept these visualizations as the truth and will make them come true in your life. Before going to sleep each night, visualize these programs and continue this in order to reinforce all these positive suggestions. Again, be very aware of money and treat it with respect. In your wallet keep the denominations of the bills separated and all in neat and orderly fashion. This will cause you to be less careless of the money you have. This provides another way of reinforcing the growing respect for money and will also prevent you from being careless and wasteful. Instead of frivolous spending, you will be thinking of ways of saving this capital for an investment that will earn you more money.

After constant repetition of the positive hypnotic suggestions your inner mind will have formed plans to cooperate with your belief in financial independence. It will begin prompting you to certain actions, which will lead to the goal you have implanted in your subconscious mind. Cooperate with these promptings even though you have no conscious understanding of where they are leading.

Maybe you will feel an urge to contact someone in particular. Possibly you will feel like reading or rereading a certain book, or going to a certain place. Just do whatever strongly occurs to you, because the inner mind has been finding the solutions to the achievement of your goal.

One thing is certain. When you perform the programming and reinforcement activities in a consistent fashion you will find yourself working smarter not harder. You will find the work more interesting and enjoyable. At the same time you will be reaching your financial goals. In many cases the original goals you set will be surpassed and you will look back on them as being rather minor. Then you will realize that the time has arrived to establish newer and higher goals and following the same procedures, achieve them as well. Remember that your inner computer holds 88% of the capacity of your mental power. Whatever the subconscious mind truly believes determines what you will achieve.

In today's world, E-Commerce and the Internet have leveled the playing field for the average person to own his own business and possibly earn more money than he could ever hope for by working at a regular job. If you would like to have more quality time with your family and be in control of your own income, I suggest you read the book, Dream-Biz.com, by Burke Hedges. This is the most exciting new concept of the current Internet opportunities I have ever read. I really believe there are more opportunities available to people with a desire for financial success than ever before in the history of the world.

Discover a business that develops residual income for you. This type of business keeps growing and providing an increasing source of revenue, even while you sleep. There are many such opportunities on the Internet, which require very little investment and permit you to grow at your own pace in your spare time. In this system of interactive marketing you are relieved of bookkeeping, payroll, and merchandise stocking along with all the other headaches of running a traditional type of business. If you wish to acquire wealth, I suggest you examine such opportunities. In the following, I have listed some Internet links to helpful pages I have used successfully.

Internet Opportunities

One such company I recommend is:

MLMBigfish.com/cgi-bin/t.cgi/123236.

This site contains excellent training as well as a program to earn money right away. Just click your browser on each of the topics and read all about it. This company teaches you how to market both on and off The Internet. It guards you from all the pitfalls while teaching you how to succeed. You are guided and trained by people that have already become successful. You are supplied with an affiliate web site at no cost to you and you also get ongoing training via e-mail. Joe Shroeder has helped thousands of people to reach their financial goals. He and several of his marketing guru friends provide you with a way to achieve financial independence.

Handling a great number of inquiries requires an auto responder company, as one person just doesn't have the time to answer each individual response. You get an auto-responder, which is unlimited in the number of messages that may be sent automatically. It also stores the names and e-mail addresses of the people that contact your website. These lists are invaluable as those people develop a friendly relationship with you because you are able to contact them so quickly with prewritten answers to their questions as well as provide them with your offers. One of the best companies I have found is:

http://www.infogeneratorpro.com/index.cgi?affiliate_id=5456

Many Affiliate programs are free and can generate income for you. I have listed two such companies that have been in business a long time. They are both honest and reliable. They create personal web sites for you and offer training as well.

http://www.sixfigureincome.com/free/?132077
http://www.theduplicator.com/vip.cgi/alvin

If money and independence make you feel happy, then aim for the stars. You may miss the stars and hit the moon. People just like us are reaching the moon every day in the e-commerce business.

J. Paul Getty once said, "To become wealthy, you must own your own business." Bill Gates proved that Mr. Getty knew what he was talking about.

Chapter 18
INTERNET ROMANCE

No one would talk much in society if they knew how often they misunderstood others.

- Goethe.

If you are searching for romance, possibly a soul mate or maybe just a bit of harmless flirting, look no further. The Internet is ready, willing and able to provide you with the means to attain all of these. Before discussing romance I would like to make a few comments about the Internet experience. There are some dangers to avoid as well as some great fun to be had.

The world of computer technology and particularly the Internet never cease to amaze me. The ability to communicate in seconds with a person on the other side of the world cheaply and rapidly has opened new vistas for commerce and human understanding that boggles the mind. We now have access to every imaginable store of knowledge in the world.

This phenomenon continues to grow at such a rapid rate that it has been estimated that nearly fifty thousand new users are added each week, with no end in sight.

You can shop for automobiles, clothing and technical equipment. You are able to learn of the latest developments in medicine and even get the latest news, sports and weather reports throughout the world.

Of course, along with this valuable information you can also be deluged with advertising, pornography and many offers of possibly shady investment opportunities. The personal computer, much like microwave ovens in the 1970's, is fast becoming a necessity in the home. You are able to store names, addresses, birth dates, phone numbers, business appointments, bank statements, tax returns, mortgage information, ad infinitum. Your computer is also exposed to the possible infection of viruses designed to steal your passwords and personal information. Unruly people called hackers develop viruses. These people are obviously extremely intelligent with computers and their programs. They cause so many problems for businesses as well as for the average Internet users that they should be put in jail and never allowed to go near a computer again. It seems they have nothing better to occupy their time. There are a number of companies that develop and administer virus protection and virus removal programs. If you plan to go on the Internet you should install a virus detection program first and learn how to use it. There are an average of 300 new viruses a month sent out on the Internet to make our lives miserable. The cost to the consumer is high as some of these viruses are capable of erasing your installed programs and even causing your computer to crash. Hacking is an insidious form of vandalism as it can affect millions of people in such a short time.

I picture these hackers as peculiar and destructive social outcasts that need to aggravate society in order to achieve some type of personal recognition. They must derive a degree of satisfaction from causing problems for those of us with less computer literacy.

Pandora's Box *(Internet Romance Chat Rooms)*

The subject I became most interested in focused on people. On the Internet they offer what are called chat rooms. These vary as to subject matter, age groups and so on. From sports to politics, technical assistance, and yes, even romance. I took a special interest in the interaction of people in these chat rooms. For several months I remained anonymous and just read the comments of the people in the rooms. Most servers, such as America Online, prohibit the use of profanity and explicit sexual chatter. I found that these policies were not too well regulated and there are times when some very offensive people enter the nicest chat rooms. Fortunately, you have an ignore button which keeps their messages off your screen. There are means by which parents may keep their children from being exposed to vulgar language and access to the pornography constantly offered. Since first entering into the world of the Internet chat rooms and being able to meet some very fine people I have been truly rewarded.

Some of the rooms are specifically for technical assistance and the people who frequent these rooms are very knowledgeable and eager to help beginners learn to use their PC's.

One of the most amazing facets of the Internet chat, to me, pertained to the ways people got to know each other by recognizing their screen names. The screen name provides you with an Internet identity, or pseudonym, which you can assign yourself when you first go on the Internet. Your screen name must be unique, consisting usually of a combination of letters and numbers.

When you enter a chat room of your choice the room's host announces your name. Off to one side are the names of the people currently in that room. By clicking the mouse button on a person's screen name you are able to see their profile (if they chose to create one).

The profile may contain the person's real name, sex, marital status, date of birth, location, occupation, hobbies etc. Many people do not create a profile, as they prefer to remain anonymous. Some people create false identities and provide erroneous information regarding age, occupation, marital status etc.

You may send an instant message to anyone in the room, which they may accept or reject. They may respond and if they do you have entered into a private conversation with that person.

Proper etiquette would be to ask the person for permission to send an instant message while still public in the chat room. Naturally, after getting to know someone else over a period of time, instant messages become commonplace among friends.

The anonymity and privacy in an instant message permits people to talk about their innermost secrets. They discuss their hopes and dreams, their shortcomings, loneliness and sadness. People open up to each other in intimate ways that they would very unlikely do, face to face.

This peril, of people giving too much information about themselves, can be one of the dangers of the Internet. Unscrupulous people could take advantage of this intimacy by gaining their confidence over a period of time.

There are some people who prey on children and older people and many police departments have trained officers in charge of monitoring the chat rooms. Many arrests have been made throughout the country as a result of these operations.

Whenever you have spent some time in a chat room you may depend on finding your e-mail full of SPAM, which consists of unsolicited advertisements and invitations to pornographic sites, where they hope to lure you into spending your money.

Hopefully the Internet will eventually ban much of this, as many young people will be exposed, without the intervention of adult controls and supervision.

I have become acquainted with a number of people from the chat rooms and, through the use of instant messages, have discussed their experiences with people they have chatted with.

Some people I have talked with have had the good fortune to get to know and meet and eventually marry a person they met on the Internet. Certainly, there were many that were totally disillusioned by unhappy and unpleasant experiences. Still, a great number of chatters have become close friends over the years. They have shared joy and sorrow and they have found people who really cared and continued to communicate with them. Even pictures can be exchanged over the net making conversations far more personal. Sharing experiences with each other about their own family and friends opens new vistas of communication for people all over the world.

Romance in the chat rooms seems to me to be a Pandora's Box. Once you enter a Romance Room you may be letting yourself in for more trouble than you ever imagined. Allowing yourself to become enamoured of someone you have never met, having no true knowledge of his or her background, character and personality, is just asking for trouble. Searching for a soul mate in the romance chat rooms is a rather dangerous pastime.

There have been a number of cases in which lonely people have arranged to meet a person they were attracted to in these chats. Some of these women were violently assaulted by the person they thought was so wonderful. Many of the people who frequent romance chat rooms are very nice but also very lonely and unhappy.

The Internet provides them with a means of conversing with other people without leaving their own homes. The romance chat room is also attractive to some very unstable personalities, a number of which are sex offenders, psychotics and con artists. If you ever decide to participate in a romance chat room, I suggest that you watch what is being said in that room and be a bit reluctant to join in. Much of the conversation is devoted to sexual innuendoes and even gets to the point of explicit sexual overtures.

Don't be deceived by the apparently nice person in the chat. He just might be worse than the ones that don't try to hide their intentions. Some of these romantic conversations have led to the divorce of a happily married person having become attracted to someone on the Internet.

Studies have shown that Internet chat rooms have become an addiction to many people. Wives and husbands carrying on a cyber love affair with a stranger over the computer is a sickness that seems to be spreading quite rapidly.

The romantic attraction to a person on the Internet is more often a wishful thinking experience taking place in ones own mind. There is some excitement generated by these clandestine conversations that may have an undesirable effect on a participant's personality. This is just playing with fire. In the movie, "You've Got Mail," Tom Hanks and Meg Ryan give you a glimpse of Internet romance ala Hollywood.

Many nice people that engage in this Internet activity would never think of entering a singles bar. I believe the Romance Chat rooms have become a virtual singles bar where you may feel safe to enter and participate in meeting people that are strangers to you. Many have permitted this new and anonymous way of meeting people to influence their own behavior in a very unhealthy way. In most cases the romantic chats are at odds with reality.

There have been happy endings for some, but these are by far in the minority. The more information you disclose about yourself, the more you are placing yourself at risk. For lonely people seeking new friends and conversations, I recommend chat rooms relating to other topics such as politics, science, technology, gardening etc. You can enjoy healthy conversations and become friends with people that frequent these chat rooms. It is far less likely to run into a troubled personality in this type of chat room. The chat rooms, while being a fun source of entertainment and an opportunity for making new friends and sharing information, still remain a hunting ground for con men and fringe lunatics. People should be extremely careful about giving out personal information.

Yes, the possibility exists for finding your soul mate there, but my advice is, "Enter at Your Own Risk." A person should just observe a chat room in action without taking part in the conversation. In this way you can better judge the type of chat room you are in and the type of people you encounter. A person could, as an example, totally misrepresent themselves on their profile as to age, location, occupation, or even sex. This poses a valid danger to be aware of.

Someone you converse with may seem very attractive to you. You may even decide to meet each other. When meeting such a total stranger you should arrange for it to be in a very public place. Take a close friend along with you and play it safe.

There are companies that, for a reasonable fee, will do a background investigation of the person you intend to meet. The background check may surprise you and also save you from a lot of misery and possible danger. If the investigation proves to be one in which your cyber friend is a really good person, you will be happy to have that information too. Reality requires that we should be fully aware of the character and traits of the other person. We should know their true habits, their friends and their families. In any relationship of a romantic nature it will pay you to take time before making such important decisions. Use your common sense. Put your emotional needs on hold and be intellectually sure of all the facts regarding your desired soul mate before permitting yourself to become so vulnerable to a person you are meeting for the first time.

Recently America Online posted a warning that if you received an instant message from a person you don't know, they might possibly have the ability to obtain your password and gain access to your computer. They could then capture all your personal information stored there. In other words they could make use of your credit card information, social security number, bank account, and so forth.

Policing of these functions will improve with time; however, I encourage you to exercise caution when using the Internet. If you have children in the home be sure to employ the parental controls provided by your Internet server.

If typing out your thoughts and aspirations makes you happy, then by all means, get on the net and have a great time. You will meet new people as often as you like, day or night. Some of these will have the same interests as you. Once you have become fairly well known, you will get instant messages, frequently from those that know you and some who are just curious.

If you have an interesting occupation, or live in a specific area, or are single and at an age that attracts someone, you can bet they are going to get to know you. You may find someone of the opposite sex that interests you and that can be fun. Many people find this medium a great way of meeting people without being too shy. Dating can be arranged right over the net and if you are looking for someone to share your life with, they are out there. The best thing to do in chat rooms is to have fun. Some chatters are very witty. It can be great entertainment and for lonely people and most probably offers the safest way to have a good time. I've enjoyed chatting with people of all ages.

Recently on-line cameras have come into vogue. You can actually see the person you are conversing with while chatting. I believe that it is safer and far less expensive to meet new people on the Internet than it is by going to a singles bar. You can find out a great deal about a person in a much shorter time on the net than you can in person. People are less shy and tend to ask direct questions on the Internet. These questions are often far more personal and direct than you would ask face to face.

There are ways of blocking out people who are offensive, just by pressing a few buttons. You can also create a "buddy list" of your Internet friends. In this way you can tell when they are on-line and even send them instant messages. In the instant messages people are able to carry on private conversations. This saves a lot of money on telephone bills and is far speedier than the U.S. Postal Service.

Be cautious when using the chat rooms but don't be afraid to have fun.   <u>BE HAPPY.</u>

Chapter 19
RUBBING YOUR MAGIC LAMP

*I never know what I think about something until I read
what I've written on it.*

- William Faulkner

This chapter contains one of the most powerful secrets known to man. Read it with an open mind and apply its teaching, for it offers a sure way to get your hearts desire. The premise might be considered so simple that most scholars would scoff at it. The wisdom contained comes from a secret I came across many years ago and almost forgot. This in no way detracts from the methods I have shown you, rather it merely in a profound way simplifies what I have already discussed. There may be a connection with the universal mind, if there is such a thing. What I do know is, this method works.

Short Introduction

According to the great Greek philosopher, Socrates: *"As all nature is akin and the soul has learned all things, there is no difficulty in its eliciting or learning out of a single recollection, for all learning is but recollection."* Socrates showed his student, Plato, that this belief was true.

He called on a young untutored boy and by using skillful questioning, without giving the answer; he had the young lad solve an abstruse geometrical problem.

How could this happen? Socrates said that the boy already had this knowledge within himself. Without any instruction, the boy was able to recover that knowledge for himself, through the questions posed to him by Socrates.

How was Socrates, without the benefit of any scientific instruments, able to describe the atom so accurately, just by the reasoning of his own mind?

The German writer Ludwig Boerne, in the following essay, is probably the one who led to Sigmund Freud's discovery of modern psychoanalysis. Read the short essay by Boerne quoted here.

The Art of Becoming an Original Writer in Three Days

"There are men and books that teach Latin, Greek or French in three days, and bookkeeping in only three hours. So far, however, no one has offered a course in How To Become a Good Original Writer in three days. And yet, it's so easy! There is nothing to learn, but plenty to unlearn: nothing to acquire, but much to forget. The minds and books of today's writers are like those old manuscripts where you first have to scratch off the boring disputations of a church step-father or the mumblings of a monk before you get down to a Roman classic. Every human mind is born with beautiful ideas- new ideas too, since in every human being the world is created anew.

But life and education write their useless stuff all over them and cover them up. To see things as they really are, consider this: We know an animal, a fruit, a flower in their true shape; they appear to us the way they are. But, would anyone understand the true nature of a chicken, an apple tree, or a rose if he knew only chicken pie, applesauce, or the rose perfume? And yet that's all we ever get in the sciences and in anything that we take in through our minds rather than our senses. It comes to us changed and made over; we never get to know it in its raw naked form. Thinking is the kitchen where all truths are killed, plucked, cut up, fried, and pickled. What we need most today are unthinking books- books with things in them rather than thoughts.

There are only a very few original writers. Our best writers differ from the poorer ones far less than you might think. One writer creeps to his goal, another runs, a third hobbles, a fourth dances, a fifth drives, and a sixth rides on horseback: but the goal and the road are common to all. Great new ideas are found only in solitude: but where is solitude to be found? You can get away from people-and at once you are in the noisy marketplace of books; you can throw away the books too; but how do you clear the mind of all the conventional ideas that education has poured into it? The true art of self training is the art of making yourself ignorant: the finest and most useful of the arts but one that is rarely and poorly practiced. In a million people there are only a thousand thinkers and in a thousand thinkers only one self thinker.

People today are like gruel, kept in shape only by the pot; you find hardness and firmness only in the crust, the lowest layer of the people; and gruel stays gruel-if a golden spoon scoops out a mouthful, it tears relatives apart but does not end relationships.

The true search for knowledge is not like the voyage of Columbus but like that of Ulysses. Man is born abroad, living means seeking your home, and thinking means living. But the home of ideas is the heart; if you want fresh water, you must draw from that source; the mind is but a river, on whose banks live thousands who muddy its waters by washing, bathing, flax steeping, and other dirty business. The mind is the arm, the heart is the will. Strength can be acquired, increased and trained; but what good is strength without the courage to use it? A cowardly fear of thinking curbs us all; the censorship of public opinion is more oppressive than that of governments. Most writers are no better than they are because they have ideas but no character. Their weakness comes from vanity. They want to surpass their fellow writers; but to surpass someone you must meet him on his own ground, to overtake someone you must travel the same road. That's why good writers have so much in common with bad ones; the good one is like the bad one but a little bigger; he goes in the same direction but a little farther.

To be original you must listen to the voice of your heart rather than the clamor of the world-and have the courage to teach publicly what you have learned.

The source of all genius is sincerity; men would be wiser if they were more moral. And now follows the application that I promised: Take several sheets of paper and for three days in succession, without any pretense or hypocrisy, write down everything that comes to your mind. Write what you think about yourself, about women, about the Turkish War, about Goethe, about the Fonk Trial, about the Last Judgment, about your boss- and after three days you will be beside yourself with surprise at all the new, unheard of ideas you had. That's the art of becoming an original writer in three days!"

As silly as this essay may have seemed to you, it contains the secret of unlocking the true power of your subconscious mind. That vast inner computer, I have continually referred to throughout this book, contains more wisdom and knowledge than you can ever imagine. The practice of writing the dictation's to your conscious mind, by the subconscious, will allow you to develop more rapidly in your ability to unleash this great inner power. Do not be concerned about where the promptings lead you in your writing. Just sit down and place on paper whatever comes into your mind without any concern as to grammar, punctuation or syntax. Get yourself a legal pad and a reliable pen and write and write and write. Best results usually come when we do this after a good night of sleep. But whatever time you decide on, just sit down and let the writing flow.

You will be greatly surprised by the revelations that will pour out onto the paper. You will learn many secrets about yourself and your own nature. You may even discover solutions to problems that may have plagued you in the past. You might just have your inner mind show you the way to become wealthy. You could possibly become a great writer. The potential benefits remain limitless.

There is a great deal to be said about writing thoughts and ideas down on paper. One of the greatest teachers of our time is Napoleon Hill. He said, "Reduce your plan to writing. The moment you complete this, you will have definitely given concrete form to the intangible desire."

I have discovered that planning my daily activities on paper not only works as a reminder but also helps me see which activities are the most important to accomplish. This also assists in time management, helping to organize the things most important for me to give priority to, arranging them in a sequence that reduces waste motion.

Committing your goals to paper not only helps you to clarify and analyze them, but additionally, programs these goals into your subconscious mind. While not as effective as the hypnotic visualization programming, it definitely acts as a powerful reinforcement tool for the hypnotic suggestions you have worked on.

The more time you devote to writing, the more orderly and clear your own thinking becomes. Writing longhand has a far more direct effect on your psyche than typing on a machine or computer. The ideomotor activity of the muscles appears to be very closely tied to the mental activity involved in writing. It is far superior to verbally dictating to a recording machine.

Even if you only spend fifteen minutes a day at writing your thoughts down, you will greatly benefit from this exercise. While our thoughts may not be transmitted clearly to others this way, they become far more lucid to us. No one needs to read your jottings, they are meant for your own private use.

Diaries, written by famous people from the past, give us wonderful perceptions of their personalities and character. This is enhanced by the observations made by handwriting analysts. These additional insights are probably more revealing than the actual content of the diaries.

In reading comments of famous writers who attempted to describe the way they wrote, I discovered a great many just started writing and let the story unfold itself before their eyes, without any conscious plan or effort. They really didn't know how they created the books they had written.

I have called this chapter, Rubbing Your Magic Lamp. The rubbing is the writing, the paper is the lamp, and the Genie of the lamp reveals itself as your own subconscious mind.

Your subconscious mind already has all the answers you need to be a happy and successful person. You must merely tap into it and all that it has to offer.

This chapter would be incomplete if I overlooked the science of Graphology, (the observation and interpretation of handwriting). The study of handwriting continues to make great strides, especially in Europe. Our handwriting is a result of the motor impulses of the person writing longhand. Muscles and nerves react to conscious and subconscious stimuli. The famous French scientists, Dr. Pierre Janet and Professor Charles Henry, conducted exhaustive tests of handwriting, which took place at The Sorbonne from 1929 through 1931. These tests proved that our handwriting reflects our physical, emotional and mental states. Handwriting analysis has become a science with which therapists can decipher emotional and mental states based on classified knowledge. Handwriting affords a very direct route to contacting and also influencing the subconscious mind. Through the findings of these renowned pioneers, the practice of Graphotherapeutics was developed. They discovered that by changing the form and content of the patient's handwriting, they were able to directly influence the subconscious mind in order to achieve positive behavioral improvements.

The book, "Graphotherapeutics," by Paul de Sainte Colombe, is an excellent guide to the understanding and practice of this pen and pencil therapy for self-improvement.

Chapter 20
GOD SMILES

*What men usually ask for when they pray to God is, that
two and two may not make four.*

- Russian Proverb.

We should use every means available to us in our quest
for self-improvement. Many readers will have very little
interest in religion, but the majority of people do believe in
the existence of a Supreme Being. No matter what religion
you may belong to, they all tell us to pray. More than that,
we are told to pray with faith and true belief that our prayers
will be answered. Prayers should be directed toward the
end result we desire without telling God how to bring this
about.

When we ask for good things, not only for ourselves
but for others as well, and believe that the good results will
come about, our prayers will have more efficacy.

If we are expecting immediate results, we might be
disappointed, because that is not the usual way that prayers
are answered. Rather, persistence and true belief in the
outcome normally proves more effective.

If our prayer remains simple and directed at a result that
would be beneficial to others and ourselves, the answers
will become apparent in time. Belief must be prerequisite
to effective prayer. If we harbor doubts or feelings of guilt
or unworthiness, we tend to nullify the objective of our
prayer.

For religious people, prayer should be coupled with
good works and a happy positive attitude. Too often people
pray with a negative attitude, feeling themselves unworthy
of even voicing the good results they want to receive. This

approach to prayer will be self-defeating. I believe God helps us to help ourselves to reach the happier life we desire. Prayer also reinforces the positive suggestions we have programmed into our minds. The real believed expectations in our prayers are a positive force for improving our lives and the lives of those around us.

It seems extremely difficult not to believe in a Universal Mind. Whether you call that mind God or Allah, or Jehovah, the intelligence shown in the design of the human body, with all the intricacies of the nervous system, the organs and musculature, lead us to realize that we are not just an accident of nature. Coupled with all the observations of nature and the universe, these all tend to indicate the existence of a supreme intelligence. Whether you believe in God or not, the entire Universe cries out for the conclusion that a supreme intelligence exists and that intelligence continues to express itself not only through religion but also through the very tangible reality of nature.

The more science delves into the wonders of the universe the more it discovers that we have only begun to scratch the surface of knowledge.

We are constantly finding more universes beyond universes. Conversely, in the microcosm, we are discovering more universes within the universe of atomic structure. The more we learn, the more questions arise. The prouder we become, the more we are humbled, and God smiles.

The great religions of the world all have one basic commonality:

What is hateful to you; do not to your fellow man. That is the entire law; all the rest is commentary.

- Judaism.

Hurt not others in ways that yourself find hurtful.

- Buddhism.

If there is one principle, which ought to be acted upon throughout one's life, surely it is that of loving-kindness. Do not unto others what you would not have them do unto you.

- Confucianism.

In everything, do unto others, as you would have them do unto you.

- Christianity.

None of you is a believer until he desires for his brother that which he desires for himself.

- Islam.

Blessed is he who prefers his brother before himself.

- Baha'i.

The effectiveness of prayer is aided by our living in a kind, loving and forgiving manner. God smiles whenever one of us does an act of kindness toward another human being, especially when we help the outcasts of society. Being omnipotent, He sees all, even the kind actions done in secret.

Why are we moved so personally by the lives of people like Mother Teresa, of Calcutta, Dr. Tom Dooley and numerous others who have opened their hearts and minds to the needs of the poor, sick, wretched and imprisoned of the world? Do we recognize a godlike love of others in the way they served humanity?

We are always the richer for helping those that cannot repay and, most especially, if we do not expect to be repaid. Giving money to help others is certainly charitable, but physically assisting those in need, constitutes a far greater act of mercy.

Los Quixotes are medical professionals, mostly Mexican-Americans, who travel at their own expense every year to Jalalpa El Grande, an overwhelmingly poor barrio in Mexico City. They stay in a convent and put in long days offering free medical care that the local people could never get otherwise. The doctors often bring family members to help.

Dr. Ricardo Rojas, a pediatrician, says, "I wanted my children never to take for granted the gifts God has given them, and I wanted them to see poverty. I wanted to create in them a generous heart by teaching them to give not just money, but service."

We must come to the realization that we resemble God in many ways, as He created us in his own image and likeness.

God is love. When we love we are coming closer to the real person that God wants us to become. God is not the dour judge, as many of us have pictured him. We are the apple of his eye, each and every one of us. Yes, God smiles, and so should we and be happy, as he would have us. If we insist, in our own pride, to decide what will prove the best for us, we make a great mistake. To have the faith of a little child in a loving God, will provide the wisest virtue we can ever obtain.

Enjoy all the gifts you already have and be willing to share them with others. Pray for wisdom. When you finally are able to know and follow his will for your life, then you will become a truly happy person.

I believe God has a tremendous sense of humor. If he did not, we would never have comedy and laughter in this life. I am sure that happiness and laughter are as necessary to life as are air and water. He may not be laughing, but I am sure that God Smiles.

Important message from a friend on the
following pages.

Memo from God

================

To: YOU
Date: TODAY
From: THE BOSS
Subject: YOURSELF
Reference: LIFE

I am GOD.

Today I will be handling all of your problems.
Please remember that I do not need your help.

If life happens to deliver a situation to you that you cannot handle, do not attempt to resolve it.

Kindly put it in the SFGTD (something for God to do) box.
It will be addressed in My time, not yours.
Once the matter is placed into the box, do not hold on to it.

If you find yourself stuck in traffic, don't despair. There are people in this world for which driving is an unheard of privilege.

Should you have a bad day at work; think of the man who has been out of work for years.

Should you despair over a relationship gone bad? Think of the person who has never known what it's like to love and be loved in return.

Should you grieve the passing of another weekend? Think of the woman in dire straits, working twelve hours a day, seven days a week, just to feed her children.

Should your car break down, leaving you miles away from assistance; think of the paraplegic who would love the opportunity to take that walk.

Should you notice a new gray hair in the mirror; think of the cancer patient in chemo who wishes she had hair to examine.

Should you find yourself at a loss and pondering what is life all about, asking what my purpose is? Be thankful. There are those who didn't live long enough to get the opportunity.

Should you find yourself the victim of other people's bitterness, ignorance, smallness or insecurities; Remember, things could be worse.

You could be them!!!!

(Your Creator...GOD)

Chapter 21
PROGRAMMING FOR SUCCESS

Decide what you want. Determine the price. Pay the price.
-Bunker Hunt.

Building a superhighway to happiness, good health, joy and success in our mind should be a daily exercise for each of us. This is called Programming. The methods will be outlined after this preface.

People respond almost instantaneously to certain neurological triggers. These responses have been learned over a period of many years and seemed to provoke appropriate feelings within us.

One of the most powerful motivations in humans is to avoid pain. While we all desire the feelings of happiness, joy, ecstasy and inner peace, we will first of all focus on the avoidance of pain.

Have you noticed your moods change throughout the day? Sometimes we feel blue and discouraged only later to be in a different mood such as anger, boredom, happiness etc. Mood swings are common to us all.

Understanding the chemical and electrical neuropathways in the brain as well as the powerful interaction of the physical and mental connections within each of us is not needed in order to use this program effectively. We don't need to know how a computer chip functions in order to operate a computer. It isn't necessary that we understand the internal combustion engine along with its electronic brain that governs timing, fuel injection, anti-lock brakes, triggers for air bags etc. in order to drive our own cars. We don't need to comprehend all these things in order to use them.

The fact is that the human brain and body are infinitely more complex than any computer, automobile, space vehicle or any other man made machine in existence. Let's use the least complicated way to describe the function of the brain and its effect on our physical body, our feelings and our actions.

Our brains consist of billions of cells, which are connected to each other by millions of neurological pathways. These pathways are carrying messages constantly. The more frequently the identical messages travel along the various paths the faster and easier these messages are transferred. In many cases the messages being communicated result in triggering unpleasant feelings and responses.

At some point in our life these responses seemed appropriate and the more often these conditioned responses occurred the stronger and more ingrained they became.

There was always a reason or reward associated with these response messages. We became conditioned to avoid touching a hot iron or placing our hands too close to a flame. These are learned responses based on experience and have become useful for our own protection and survival. Other than the fear response to loud noises or the feeling of falling, infants as they grow older learn to respond to stimuli in various ways. Many of these responses are inappropriate and harmful.

We learn to develop moods such as sadness, frustration, grief and fear as well as happiness, elation, confidence, peace etc. as a result of stimuli outside ourselves so our perceptions of these determine the way we react and feel. Because we all have different perceptions we seem to develop different reactions to stimuli than many other people have. What one man may embrace may be the thing that would terrify another.

In our society we have become inclined to many negative states, which in turn provoke feelings of unhappiness and distress. In order to lessen the pain of these emotions we develop coping habits to at least temporarily overcome the unpleasant feelings. Escapes such as alcohol, drugs, overeating, oversleeping and so forth provide a short-term release.

As these behaviors become reinforced by repetition, the neuropathways send messages that trigger these actions more frequently and more rapidly.

Humans genetically will be motivated more strongly to avoid pain than to gain pleasure. For this reason many resort to the temporary and harmful escape behaviors we just mentioned. Since these activities are harmful to us we need to use other means to overcome the unwanted feelings and produce happy, joyful and uplifting emotional states within ourselves.

We have the power to control our thoughts and are in the position of being able to change the way we feel emotionally. We can override and discard our old unwanted feelings and responses and moods.

The important thing to realize is that we possess the ability to change our beliefs and perceptions in order to achieve happy, positive and empowering responses. In addition to this we have the powerful ability to rid ourselves of the old negative beliefs, feelings and behaviors.

My attempt at condensing his techniques for self-improvement will sound simple. These programs coupled with the application of self-hypnosis produce excellent results without the need to know all the hows and whys these methods are effective.

The practices we will discuss have been around for a very long time. Much of this understanding is based on the work of Alfred Kaczynski. His book "Science and Sanity" written in 1933, was studied and applied by many therapists quite successfully. A quotation from Korzybski and citations of Science and Sanity in their book "The

Structure of Magic" indicate that Bandler and Grinder are familiar with general semantics (Korzybski's work). They, (Bandler and Grinder) also cite by name, Virginia Satir and Fritz Perls, who themselves have acknowledged a debt to Korzybski.

A very important program for changing ourselves for the ideals of success and happiness is to acknowledge the fact that the mind and the body are totally linked together. The way we act, look, move and behave as well as our own physical posture, facial expressions and physical conditioning have a direct influence on our moods, emotions and behaviors. To learn more about this important facet of total improvement I recommend you read and employ the methods taught by Bill Phillips in his best selling book, "Body for Life." Harper, Collins Publishers.

We will be focused on explaining the methods of mental reprogramming with the emphasis on simplicity.

The key to power is taking action. Most of our feelings are influenced and triggered by subconscious programming. We respond to events and stimuli by entering a pre-prepared state. This is a feeling we have learned to enter by our actions, thoughts and beliefs that have been ingrained over a long period of time.

Our beliefs have a direct effect on our attitudes and feelings. Believing we will fail at reaching our goals will insure failure. Fortunately we have the power to direct our minds to change what we believe from negative (harmful) to positive (empowering). There are many ways we can do this.

First, make an examination of what beliefs in your own mind are obstacles to reaching the goals you want to achieve. List these beliefs you hold and then assign them a priority of importance.

The next step is to list the beliefs of happy and successful people you know or that you have read about and see how they differ from the beliefs that have been obstacles to your own happiness and success.

Spend some deep, soul-searching time at this. Be very honest with yourself as replacing the hindering beliefs with empowering beliefs is the road to your own self-fulfillment. Feelings or states are a result of conditioned response as well as physical circumstances such as an illness or an injury.

It takes time to recover from a physical illness. Treatments, rest and medicines assist our body to fully rebound from a physical sickness or injury. We can greatly assist the healing process by positive and happy thinking. The body and mind are so closely connected that each has a powerful influence on the other. Words have such a profound effect on our lives that we should all learn to choose them well in our self-talk and our conversations with others.

Doctors should use words that build up their patients rather than saying things that might well deprive them of any hope of recovery. Morbid words tend to demoralize people and do have a profoundly negative effect on their immune systems. The use of empowering, uplifting words have been proven to be highly effective in stimulating the patient's immune system to fight and overcome illness. The modern doctor's bedside manner has become more enlightened in this regard. He will definitely become a better healer.

You can actually make yourself feel happier and more energetic by physically smiling; laughing and maintaining a powerful erect physical posture. This physical behavior sends positive healthy commands to the brain that alter an unhealthy, unhappy mood into one of well being and joy.

Unhappy feelings as a result of our own thinking and self-talk can be replaced with happy healthy feelings just by changing the way we think. As Korzibski said, "The map is not the territory," so our perception of a circumstance may be totally wrong.

What we believe about anything is our own map and our map can be realistically redrawn to produce the feelings, emotions and results we desire.

When a person is physically ill, feeling abandoned or financially bankrupt they still have the ability to produce feelings of happiness and confidence. They might read a humorous book, watch comedy shows and movies on T.V. and have enjoyable conversations with other people. It is important to visualize being healthy and successful using one's own mind for that purpose. All of these exercises have the capability of stimulating the patient's immune system to more effectively fight the illness. These exercises also rebuild a persons flagging confidence to the point of total belief in success physically, emotionally and financially.

Feelings are our physical and emotional states triggered by words, thoughts and visualizations. The feelings are merely conditioned responses to these triggers.

When we are feeling depressed or frightened we are responding to the sights, sounds and emotions that were connected to this state. By examining the unpleasant memories that influenced these unwanted feelings we will recognize the senses that were the most powerful keys to producing these states and use these same keys to overcome this inappropriate condition.

We can choose the way we feel through our ability to direct our brain with visual, oral, mental and physical commands.

If the key is visual we can in our mind cause the negative picture to become hazy and indistinct, even to the point of making it disappear. We can make it dim and small while at the same time visualizing the happy experience as being bright and large and powerful. With repetition the unpleasant feeling will be linked with and overpowered by the pleasant, happy feeling.

If the key is related to sounds, we can cause the sounds to become merely whispers, which eventually become silence. Here again causing the happy sounds to be louder and clearer they too will become linked to the unwanted and weak sounds and therefore the unwanted sounds become triggers to elevate the mood to the happier state.

If thoughts are the most powerful key, we can challenge the thought saying to ourselves that this particular belief is false. We should imagine that the unwanted thought is very small and very weak. In our mind we tower over the thought and command it to automatically change into a belief that makes us feel happy and secure. In time the detrimental belief will actually become the trigger for the new and positive belief.

We can decide to feel great and happy and successful. Total belief in your own right and ability to choose is developed and programmed into the conscious and subconscious mind.

Continual reaffirmation will give you the power to create your own state of feeling at will. The more of the senses used in this conditioning process, the sooner you will be in control of your life and your emotions.

One of the wisest things you can do is to learn how happy and successful people think and behave. Read all you can about the ones you respect and would like to emulate. Discover not only what they did but also how they did it. The sequence of thought and action is very important. Concentrate on all the thoughts and traits that made them become the person you would like to be.

The world is full of excellent role models. If you know someone personally like this, ask them to help you to develop your thinking and actions to resemble them. You can literally approach nearly anyone. People love to talk about themselves. They like to teach others and they will usually respond in a very positive way to you. If you want to be a winner, talk to a winner. Discover what was important to them and how they were able to achieve their goals. You must not only think the way they did but you must also take action.

Many people are gifted with the ability of clear visualization. You can actually learn to see yourself in situations you create in your mind.

You can see yourself just as you would like to be. You can place yourself in any lifestyle you wish and behave accordingly. Since you are in total command of the scene you virtually write the script and act out the role until your mind accepts this as reality. Your subconscious mind will then prompt you to do all the things needed to cooperate with this newly perceived reality. This practice is most effective when done in a mild state of hypnosis. Daily repetition convinces the mind that this is the way you truly are.

As mentioned earlier in this book, we have a wonderful tool, the tape recorder. Using our own voice we record new beliefs about ourselves. These new beliefs cause excellent changes in our attitudes. As our attitudes change, they in turn will cause us to have greater more positive feelings.

Feelings will then lead us into appropriate actions that will produce the positive results we seek. In chapter 6, the chapter regarding stopping smoking, I gave a number of suggestions that could be recorded and played back. As I said then, the suggestions there are a fine start for stopping smoking messages. However, the best results will be achieved when you personally choose your own statements to be applied to whatever goal you wish to accomplish. These statements should reflect what it is that you want do, and also statements to the effect that you know you will succeed in achieving your goal. Once you have written down the suggestions you feel will point you in the right direction, begin recording. When finished with the recording, make a constant effort to replay these words over and over. It is not necessary to pay close attention to the messages as the inner ear will transmit the information directly to the subconscious mind.

My contract with you is to place you in the WINNING ZONE to reap all of its benefits.

****

By using hypnosis and vivid visualization of our desired outcome as already having been achieved we are able to direct into the brain those beliefs and habit patterns more rapidly, powerfully and with lasting results. You will soon find yourself living life in the confident, happy manner you have chosen. The methods I've listed throughout the book are time tested, efficient and simple. Best of all they work and work well. They quickly become good habits to follow.

****

Epilogue

This book has been my effort to condense many ideas and effective programs into a guide that will help you enjoy life more fully. The fact that it simplifies subjects that could fill a small library should not detract from its value. The homespun, common sense approach, while sounding a bit unscholarly, is just my way of communicating the valuable lessons I have learned and continue to teach.

The underlying power, I have stressed, is _belief._ What a person truly believes about himself or herself is what that person will surely adhere to. You can rewrite your mental script. Your inner beliefs will then conform to the goals and desires you wish to achieve. You now have the tools to program your inner mind to your own chosen goals. You possess the power to control your thoughts and beliefs in order to become a happy, successful person. Develop a compassion for others and acceptance of yourself. Become the best person you can possibly imagine. Remember, in order to achieve your goals, you must definitely take action. These actions will lead to positive desired results.

You will then travel your own path to success and happiness.

"THE WINNING ZONE"

Writing is very facile. Easy to read and understand. Each chapter contains valuable information and is complete in itself. An excellent confidence builder for people in all walks of life. I feel everyone will benefit by using the programs explained in this book. The improvement in the efficiency and attitude of our employees as a result of using Smith's programs has been astounding.

Amarc International.

Powerful words from an obviously gentle spirit. I am inspired and moved enough to suggest that anyone who wants to look within, to find courage and motivation, should begin with this book of life. Al Smith does not give definition to what is right or wrong in the world...just what is! Use it to make the most of your world. The opportunity to gain from the experience and wisdom of this author is his gift to us.

Jeanne Kearns
(Golf Professional)

About the Author

This book is for everyone wishing to improve the quality of his or her life in terms of happiness and success. The programs the author describes in this book are based mainly on the training he received through The Hypnosis Motivation Institute in Tarzana, California. Prior to his becoming a certified hypnotherapist he had applied his energies mainly in the field of sports psychology. Mr. Smith worked directly with Al Geiberger and James Blakely in the sport of golf and with many other outstanding athletes in the sports of football, baseball and basketball. Alvin Smith was the sports psychology, contributing editor for Golf Illustrated Magazine for many years and also contributed to a golf instructional videotape starring Al Geiberger. He expanded his training in order to help people with weight reduction, overcoming harmful habits, and improvement in self-esteem. He trained groups of salespeople to apply these methods to achieve their goals and improve their quality of life. Smith truly cares about helping others to constantly improve themselves through the application of these methods he teaches. Most of what he says deals directly with our everyday concerns. Mr. Smith has reduced the very technical thinking and training of the psychologists to an easy to understand and apply method for the average person to change his or her life for the better.

Stephen M. Smith, B.S.
Business Administration,
Organizational Systems Management
Cal State University, Northridge, CA.

www.ingramcontent.com/pod-product-compliance
Lightning Source LLC
Chambersburg PA
CBHW022210050726
47590CB00002B/724